Babylonian Mythology

DON NARDO

LUCENT BOOKS

A part of Gale, Cengage Learning

GALE
CENGAGE Learning

Detroit • New York • San Francisco • New Haven, Conn • Waterville, Maine • London

LIBRARY OF CONGRESS CATALOGING-IN-PUBLICATION DATA

Nardo, Don, 1947-
  Babylonian mythology / by Don Nardo.
     pages. cm. -- (Mythology and culture worldwide)
  ISBN 978-1-4205-0832-1 (hardcover)
  1. Mythology, Assyro-Babylonian. I. Title. II. Series: Mythology and culture worldwide.
  BL1620.N37 2013
  299'.21--dc23

                                                          2012014088

Lucent Books
27500 Drake Rd.
Farmington Hills, MI 48331

ISBN-13: 978-1-4205-0832-1
ISBN-10: 1-4205-0832-6

Printed in the United States of America
2 3 4 5 6 7 16 15 14 13

TABLE OF CONTENTS

Map of Mesopotamia   4
Family Tree of Major Babylonian Gods   5
Major Characters in Babylonian Mythology   6

Introduction
No Sense of History   7

Chapter 1
Babylonian Preservation of Gods and Myths   13

Chapter 2
Searching for the Beginnings of Things   32

Chapter 3
Quests for the Secrets of Immortality   47

Chapter 4
The Inevitability of Conflict and Calamity   62

Chapter 5
Babylonian Myths' Impact on Western Society   77

Notes   93
Glossary   96
For More Information   97
Index   99
Picture Credits   103
About the Author   104

Map of Mesopotamia

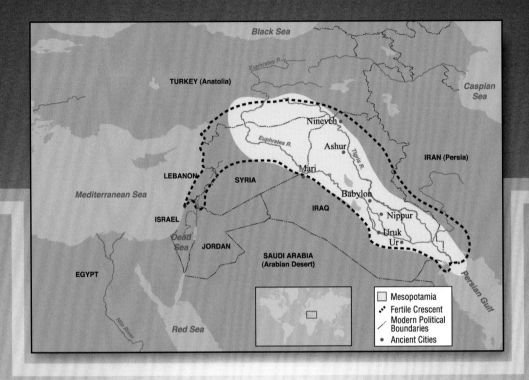

Family Tree of Major Babylonian Gods

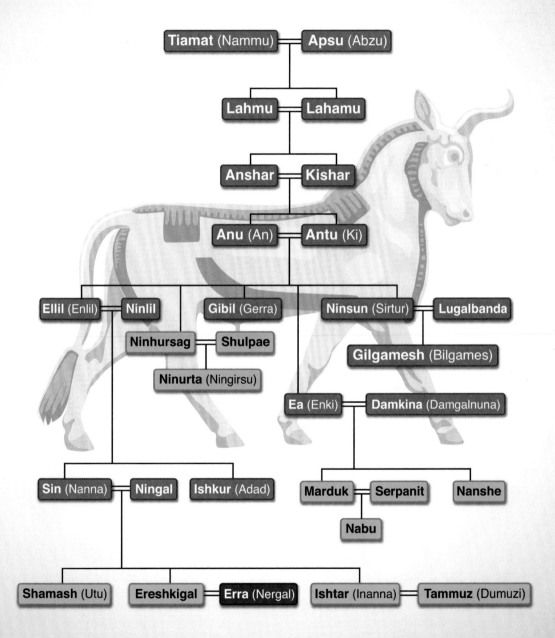

Major Characters in Babylonian Mythology

Character Name	Pronunciation	Description
Adapa	(uh-DAH-puh)	A Babylonian wise man who attempted to obtain immortality.
Anu	(AY-noo)	An early Babylonian god who was seen as a sort of father figure for the other gods.
Atrahasis	(ah-trah-HAH-sis)	A Babylonian wise man who was warned by a god to build a large boat because a great flood was imminent.
Ea	(AY-ah)	The god of freshwater, who was also known for his wisdom and as a protector of the crafts and craftspeople.
Ellil	(EL-il)	As the Sumerian Enlil, he was the chief god of earthly affairs, but as the Babylonian Ellil, he had lesser authority because under the Babylonians, Marduk had assumed most of his major duties.
Enkidu	(EN-ki-doo)	The wild man who becomes Gilgamesh's best friend in the *Epic of Gilgamesh*.
Ereshkigal	(ay-RESH-ki-gal)	The grim goddess of the dark Underworld.
Erra	(AIR-uh)	An aggressive war god who delights in fighting and destroying cities.
Gilgamesh	(GIL-guh-mesh)	The main character in the myth that bears his name, he goes on a famous quest to find the secret of eternal life.
Ishtar	(ISH-tar)	The goddess of love and sexual passion, who was also identified with the planet today called Venus.
Ishum	(ISH'm)	The god of fire and the faithful assistant of the war god Erra.
Marduk	(MAR-dook)	The supreme leader of the Babylonian gods, who defeated evil and created both the universe and human beings.
Ninhursag	(nin-HOOR-sahg)	A mother goddess who oversaw and nurtured wild animals.
Ninurta	(ni-NOOR-tah)	A deity who began as an overseer of irrigation and eventually morphed into a powerful war god.
Tiamat	(tee-AH-mut)	The goddess of salt waters who was present at the creation of the universe.

INTRODUCTION

No Sense of History

A famous hero went on a quest to find the secret of immortality, the goddess of love descended into the Underworld and became trapped there, and a man built a large boat and loaded it with animals in order to save living things from a world-destroying flood sent by the gods. These are among the major and widely recognizable myths of the ancient Babylonians. The third one, about the flood, is especially familiar today because of its similarity to the biblical tale of Noah and the ark. Like several other tales from Babylonian mythology, it has become a part of the fabric of both Middle Eastern and Western (European-based) culture and folklore.

The Sumerian Connection

The Babylonians inhabited what is now southern Iraq, northwest of the Persian Gulf, from about 1800 B.C. to roughly 550 B.C. During these centuries the mighty city of Babylon was the most prosperous, admired, and, at times, powerful city in the Middle East. Situated on the Euphrates River about 60 miles (97km) south of modern-day Baghdad, it was also the capital of several Babylonian empires that rose and fell over time in the region.

The Babylonians had a rich tradition of gods and heroes and a wide array of myths associated with them. They were among several peoples of Mesopotamia (the ancient area approximately coinciding with modern-day Iraq) whose cultures developed directly out of that of an earlier people called the Sumerians. The Sumerians dominated southern Mesopotamia in the 3000s and 2000s B.C. There, in what is now seen as one of the four cradles of civilization, they erected the world's first cities and devised the first known writing system. They also developed a rich religious tradition, with a pantheon of gods and many myths associated with those gods.

Sumerian culture, including its gods and myths, became so deeply entrenched throughout Mesopotamia and some nearby lands that it remained, in one form or another, a permanent fixture of the region. The Sumerian city-states declined and fell in the late 2000s B.C. The peoples who took over those states, however, had already absorbed Sumerian culture. So they carefully preserved and perpetuated it, just as the residents of the early United States carried on most cultural aspects of the English and other Europeans from whom they had evolved. Thus, most of the Babylonian myths were originally Sumerian myths. Scholar Jennifer Westwood elaborates on the Sumerian connection, saying:

> It is lucky for us that when the Babylonians became dominant [in Mesopotamia] they did not wipe out the Sumerian civilization, but took it over. . . . The Babylonians saw fit to preserve the Sumerian language and they used it as their language of religion, much as Latin was used by the [Christian] Church in medieval Europe. Together with the language, they took over the gods, the mythology, and the hero-legends. Indeed, most of the Sumerian texts which have been found by archaeologists, were actually written down by Babylonians when Sumerian was already a dead language. . . . So we cannot really talk of . . . Babylonian myths and legends, but to be accurate should call them something like Sumero-Babylonian. This is so clumsy, however, that most people simply speak of Babylonian myths . . . bearing in mind that many of these are of Sumerian origin.[1]

The Dawn of History

These same stories could just as well be termed "Sumero-Assyrian" myths. This is because the peoples who inhabited northern Mesopotamia, which was generally called Assyria in ancient times, also inherited Sumerian culture, gods, and myths. In fact, the Babylonian and Assyrian cultures were closely linked. Both used dialects of a single language, Akkadian, the first major language to replace Sumerian in the region. (Northern Mesopotamia was also referred to in a general way as Akkad, based on a city of that name that was prominent in the area in the 2000s B.C. A king named Sargon

An Akkadian cuneiform tablet praises King Sargon. Both the Babylonian and Assyrian cultures spoke and wrote dialects of the Akkadian language, which replaced Sumerian in northern Mesopotamia.

of Akkad, who reigned from about 2340 to 2284 B.C., created the world's first empire.)

Because the first modern translations of Mesopotamian mythical tales were taken from Akkadian texts, those versions became the most famous. Over time they were translated not only into English, but also French, Spanish, German, Russian, and numerous other tongues. The same situation prevailed in the ancient Middle East, as archaeologist Stephanie Dalley explains:

> Akkadian myths and epics were universally known during antiquity [ancient times]. And they were not restricted to the Akkadian language. Some were definitely told in Sumerian, Hittite, Hurrian, and Hebrew. The story itself flourishes beyond the boundaries of any particular language or ethnic group. This happened partly because Akkadian was the language of diplomacy throughout the ancient [Middle] East from the mid-second to mid-first millennium B.C., even in Egypt, Anatolia [what is now Turkey], and Iran. Trainee scribes in those far-flung countries practiced their skills on Akkadian literary texts. Also . . . strong nomadic and mercantile [business-related] elements in the population traveled enormous distances [and] trading colonies abroad were [numerous]. Therefore, Akkadian stories share a common ground with tales in the Old Testament, the [Greek epic poems] the *Iliad* [and] the *Odyssey* . . . and the *Arabian Nights*. They were popular with an international audience at the dawn of history.[2]

Connecting Present and Past

It is important to emphasize that phrases like "dawn of history" and indeed the very idea of history as a progression of events accompanied by change and advancement is strictly a modern concept. The Babylonians and the other ancient peoples with whom they interacted lacked this sense or view of history. They did not have a science of archaeology, in which experts systematically dig up and study past peoples and artifacts. Nor did they envision that things would be any different in the future. They simply "did not think in terms of history," says the noted English Assyriologist H.W.F. Saggs. (An Assyriologist is a scholar who specializes in ancient Mesopotamian peoples and cultures.) Saggs explains:

> They saw their institutions and way of life not as developments from more primitive forms, but rather as something which the gods had decreed in the beginning and which had existed unchanged forever. With no concept of social progress, they had no incentive to make a conscious record of life in the thousand years before 2500 B.C., when some of the most momentous advances in human society were taking place.[3]

This is why the Sumerians, Babylonians, Assyrians, and other ancient peoples who lived in the second millennium B.C. did not write formal history texts. That cultural advance did not occur until the rise of classical Greek culture in the middle of the first millennium B.C. The first true history books were penned by the Greek writers Herodotus, Thucydides, and Xenophon.

In place of such texts, earlier peoples cultivated their collections of myths. These tales explained how the world and heavens had come into being at the hands of divine forces and beings. They also told how humans originated, also through the intervention of the gods. Once those deities had created the human race, it was believed that human civilization and institutions would continue in more or less the same form virtually forever. The major myths remained a vital link to people's origins, so it was crucial to perpetuate those myths. Hence, the Babylonians preserved the main Sumerian myths, along with Sumerian gods and religious customs.

The manner of this preservation was at first strictly oral. But later the myths were written down, mostly in the form of epics, long stories penned in verse. According to University of Windsor scholar Stephen Bertman:

> Before writing's invention, such tales were recited orally, each storyteller transmitting a traditional narrative core that grew by creative embellishment [adding new

details]. Writing tended to fix [make permanent] the story's structure and content, but over the course of generations even these might be reshaped, especially in the hands of a master poet, to form a work of literary art. The civilization preserved its masterpieces by copying and recopying them. But the literary masterpieces also preserved their civilization by acting as a lifeline that connected the present to the past and the spiritual guidance it could provide.[4]

Myths Bring About Order

In this way myths not only entertained the Babylonians but also helped them understand who they were as a people. At the same time, those myths ensured that each new generation would revere tradition and thereby maintain the familiar, ordered life patterns, customs, and beliefs that one's parents and grandparents had known. Indeed, an ordered life was perhaps the greatest gift the myths imparted to a new generation. As the late scholar of the ancient Middle East Samuel N. Kramer put it, "Above all, in that early time when powerful natural forces were utterly inexplicable to fearful humans, their [religion and myths] gave perspective and order to the lives of the people."[5]

The Babylonians maintained this sense of order—of knowing what to expect and enjoying the imagined security of ceaseless sameness—for dozens of generations. Eventually, as all peoples and nations must and do, they faded from the world stage. But because the Sumerians had carved their myths onto stone tablets, most of those stories survived to entertain new generations. In all likelihood, they will live on as long as there are people to read them.

CHAPTER 1

Babylonian Preservation of Gods and Myths

Babylonia was one of the most successful of all the lands in the ancient Middle East, and it remains one of the most famous. From a geographical standpoint, Babylonia made up the southern half of Mesopotamia, the "land between the rivers." This was a reference to the Tigris and Euphrates Rivers, which flowed southeastward from Assyria in northern Mesopotamia, across Babylonia, and into the Persian Gulf. Babylonia also covered roughly the same space as Sumer, the land of the Sumerians, the equally successful people who directly preceded the Babylonians. Sumer/Babylonia stretched from just north of the modern-day Iraqi city of Baghdad southward to the shores of the gulf. That area encompassed about 10,000 square miles (25,900 sq. km) overall, a bit larger than the U.S. state of Massachusetts.

At first glance this region might seem an unlikely place to give rise to a thriving civilization. The climate is very hot and arid, and the soil is dry, windswept, and lacking minerals. Moreover, the area possesses pitifully little native stone or forests that might provide building materials for towns and cities. Yet with all these disadvantages, through ingenuity and sheer determination the Sumerians, and later the Babylonians, fashioned a flourishing culture that produced some of the most prosperous cities and finest art and literature of the ancient world.

One of the first keys to this prosperity was the brilliant idea of constructing irrigation channels that diverted life-giving water from the rivers and turned the arid plains into lush landscapes with gardens and fields filled with crops. In place of stone and wood, the residents learned to bake mud and clay into bricks for houses, public buildings, and city walls. Other inventions that helped their cities and society thrive included the sailboat, the plow, the potter's wheel, the arch, the casting and smelting of copper and bronze, and writing on clay tablets. In addition to these, they developed trade networks that allowed them to import stone, tin for their bronze, gold for fine jewelry, and a wide array of luxury goods.

In addition, the Sumerians, and then the Babylonians who later replaced them as caretakers of southern Mesopotamia, developed an incredibly rich collection of religious rituals, lore, literature, and myths. These influenced or were borrowed by a number of neighboring peoples. Among them were the inhabitants of northern Mesopotamia, Palestine, and southeastern Europe, including the Hebrews and Greeks. The latter two peoples were among the founders of Western civilization. So they transmitted some of Babylonia's myths and literary ideas to the medieval and modern worlds. The myth of Noah and the flood is perhaps the most famous example.

The Rise of Babylon

Babylonia played an important role in this transmission of myths, literature, and other cultural concepts from the Sumerians to later Western societies. Babylonian scribes carefully copied and thereby preserved the old Sumerian mythical and literary tales. As they did so, they translated them from Sumerian, which by then was no longer spoken, into Akkadian, the language of Babylonia, Assyria, and Middle Eastern diplomacy in the second millennium B.C. Thus, the modern versions of these stories are largely the Babylonian ones.

A good example is the second-most famous Babylonian myth after that of the great flood—the tale of Gilgamesh, a king of the distant past who went on a heroic quest to find the secret of immortality. (The flood story was originally part

of Gilgamesh's tale, making it a sort of myth within a myth.) The first versions of this long, complex story, which were written in Sumerian in the third millennium B.C., are mostly lost. Only some scattered fragments have been found to date. But the entire Sumerian version still existed in the early second millennium B.C., when Babylonian scribes copied them, thereby creating new, slightly more detailed renderings.

Another reason that Babylonian literature and myths survived so long was that Babylonian civilization itself was very long-lived. It also interacted in complex ways with neighboring societies and peoples, impressing upon them social elements like law codes, along with its religious ideas and myths. A brief examination of Babylonia's period of prominence as a flourishing society, country, and empire demonstrates why its culture and myths were so influential.

Both Hebrews and Greeks transmitted some of Babylonia's myths to the medieval and modern worlds, among them the story of Noah's ark and the great flood.

Babylonia began as a single city-state—Babylon, situated on the Euphrates River a bit west of the old Sumerian city of Kish. Although Babylon first appeared in late Sumerian times, it remained fairly small and unimportant until about 2000 B.C. In the four centuries that followed, called the Old Babylonian period by modern scholars, the city's territory and power greatly expanded, and it became the biggest and most imposing urban center in all of Mesopotamia. Babylon also became a wealthy cultural center that attracted people far and wide and made it a highly desirable prize for conquerors. Finally, Babylon was the center of a series of Babylonian empires that rose and fell in the center of the Middle East over the course of a millennium.

Hammurabi's Achievements

The key figure in Babylon's initial rise to greatness was King Hammurabi, who ascended the local throne in about 1792 B.C. At first his aims appeared peaceful: He constructed irrigation canals and negotiated treaties of friendship with neighboring states, including Larsa, Eshnunna, and Mari. However, he soon began to pursue a more ambitious and aggressive national policy. By the mid-1750s B.C. he had conquered Larsa, Eshnunna, and Mari, as well as several Assyrian towns in the north, including Ashur.

Hammurabi's conquests continued, and in fairly short order he became the first ruler in many centuries to control all of Mesopotamia. Moreover, he cemented Babylon's reputation as a culturally splendid city for all times. By modern estimates, it became the largest city in the world under his rule. Hammurabi's reign "left a lasting impression on future generations," scholar Karen Rhea Nemet-Nejat says, "making him one of the major figures of Mesopotamian history." Moreover, he made "Babylon the recognized seat of kingship, a position that remained uncontested until the Greeks [took control of the region later]. Babylon even survived as a [premiere Mesopotamian] religious center until the first century [A.D.]"[6]

Hammurabi also created the world's most famous and influential set of laws before those later introduced by the Greeks and Romans. He ordered his scribes to carve these

The Mark of Sumerian Religion

The late, widely respected scholar of the ancient Middle East Samuel N. Kramer eloquently described the importance of Sumerian religion in the region throughout the ancient era and in later ages:

In the course of the third millennium B.C., the Sumerians developed religious ideas and spiritual concepts which have left an indelible impression on the modern world, especially by way of Judaism, Christianity, and Islam. On the intellectual level, Sumerian thinkers and sages, as a result of their speculations on the origin and nature of the universe and its modus operandi [way of working], developed a cosmology and theology which carried such high conviction that they became the basic creed and dogma of much of the ancient [Middle] East. [Meanwhile, the] Sumerian minstrels and bards, and their later heirs, the poets and scribes . . . created what is by all odds the richest mythology of the ancient [Middle] East, which cut the gods down to human size, but did so with understanding, reverence, and above all, originality and imagination.

Samuel N. Kramer. *The Sumerians: Their History, Culture, and Character.* Chicago: University of Chicago Press, 1982, p. 112.

statutes onto an 8-foot (2.4m)-high black stone that has survived. Numbering 282 in all, those edicts cover a wide variety of issues, including marriage, adoption, medical malpractice, property rights, financial transactions, regulation of trade, and personal injury. It was the most extensive law code in the world up to that time, researcher Norman Bancroft Hunt explains, "and the first to address the problems of the ordinary citizen. Based on 'an eye for an eye,' punishments were clearly defined and commensurate with [matching] the guilty party's [level of] wealth. Hammurabi set out his reasons for formulating [the laws], so 'that the strong may not oppress the weak [and] to see that justice is done for the orphan and widow.'"[7]

These laws made Babylonian society at least a bit fairer than it had been before. Also, they set an example for other cultures in the Middle East, some of which began to experiment with writing down laws of their own. In addition, over time, having such written rules made Babylonia appear more culturally advanced than most other neighboring cultures.

Myths About Past Rulers

The era of high Babylonian culture that Hammurabi ushered in also witnessed the production of fine literature. The bulk of this literature consisted of written versions of myths that had been popular in Sumerian times. Of the surviving works of this type from the Old Babylonian period are a few tablets bearing parts of the first Babylonian version of Gilgamesh's epic story. They are hard to date precisely, but the experts' best guess is that scribes, some of whom may have been alive when Hammurabi was on the throne, produced them in the late 1700s B.C. A number of scholars think that the first written version of the chief Babylonian myth of creation was also composed at this time, but if so, it has not survived. (A later version of it was found on clay tablets buried in the ruins of a library in an Assyrian city sacked in the 600s B.C.)

Justice for All

Many of the punishments for breaking Hammurabi's laws were harsh. Receiving stolen goods, for instance, along with kidnapping and breaking and entering, could be punished by the death penalty. There were sometimes exceptions, however. Often these depended on the accused person's place in the community, since Hammurabi's laws took into account the social status and wealth of a person accused of a crime. Thus, members of the highest social class, consisting of the nobles and large landowners, might receive one penalty for a given offense, while an ordinary person (by today's standards in the lower middle class) or slave might receive a different punishment for the same crime. In general, the rich and powerful were given the harshest sentences. This was likely because society held them on a pedestal to some degree and expected them to act more honestly and honorably than other people. In this way Hammurabi's system of laws was the first one known to history that attempted to make sure that all members of society were subject to justice.

An engraved black basalt stele shows Hammurabi standing before the sun god. Below in cuneiform is the Code of Hammurabi.

Myths about earlier human rulers also circulated during the time of Hammurabi and his immediate successors. Probably the most famous besides Gilgamesh, both then and now, was the tale of Sargon, king of the city-state of Akkad (or Agade). Ancient tablets known as the Sumerian King Lists, some versions of which were compiled in the Old Babylonian period, mentioned his legend, summarized here by researcher Cyril J. Gadd:

> The name Sargon means "a legitimate king verily is created." . . . A legend records that his mother was a lowly woman, [while] his father he knew not; he was born in concealment at Azupirani on the Euphrates; his mother cast him adrift on the river in a reed basket and he was discovered by Akki an irrigator, who reared him and made him a gardener; but [the love goddess] Ishtar loved [Sargon] and he became king for 55 years.[8]

Myths such as those of Sargon, Gilgamesh, and other past rulers were not seen merely as entertaining stories, as most myths are today. Because the Babylonians had no concept of history and no history books, they filled that gap with myths about heroes, wanderers, and gods. The average person assumed that these tales were all true, or at least largely so. Therefore, hearing someone recite such a story provided a description of important events and figures of bygone ages, all leading back to the creation of the world and the first humans. According to Henrietta McCall, an expert on Babylonian myths, "We cannot know exactly who was privileged enough to hear these readings. It probably depended to some extent on where they took place: at court, in temples at [religious] festivals, or even around caravan campfires. Clearly, different locations would have commanded different types of audiences."[9]

Kings Thousands of Years Old?

The Sumerian King Lists give only a rough idea of the progression of Mesopotamian rulers in the centuries before Babylonia's rise. Also, the farther back one goes in the lists, the less realistic and more mythical the entries become. For example, the earliest kings mentioned are assigned reigns lasting up to thirty thousand years or more.

A Babylonian bronze bust from circa 2200 B.C. depicts the great king Sargon.

Written Myths of the Later Babylonians

The large Babylonian realm Hammurabi had forged did not last as long as he had hoped. Following his death, poor leadership among his successors caused the empire to decline until Babylonian territory was little larger than it had been before his rise. But Babylon itself remained a great city that symbolized high culture in the Middle East, and foreign powers still saw it as a tempting prize. In about 1595 B.C. the Hittites, a people based in central Anatolia, swept down through the Tigris-Euphrates valley and seized Babylon. They were aided by the Kassites, a culturally backward hill people who had entered Mesopotamia a century before. For

A cylinder seal and imprint from Babylon's Kassite period (sixteenth to twelfth century B.C.). The Kassites aided the Hittites in conquering Babylon. Afterward, the Hittites left the Kassites in charge, and the latter immediately absorbed the local culture.

reasons that remain uncertain, the Hittites had no sooner succeeded in capturing their valuable trophy than they abandoned it. They suddenly returned to Anatolia and left the Kassites in charge of Babylon and its immediate environs.

All was not lost for Babylon and its residents, however. Awed by the local culture, the crude Kassites rapidly absorbed it. As would happen later with others who would move to that special city, in only a few decades they became "Babylonianized" in their dress, speech, and religion. That they inherited Sumero-Babylonian myths as well is known because their scribes produced a new round of written editions of these stories in the Babylonian dialect of Akkadian. Of these, an important surviving example is a version of the Gilgamesh myth recorded by a scribe named Sin-lequ-unnini in about 1200 B.C. It was not long after these myths were recorded once more that control of Babylon fell to a series of unremarkable non-Kassite kings, most hailing from Babylonia itself or neighboring regions. In the 900s B.C. the city and surrounding region came under the domination of the Assyrians, who in the next three centuries created a powerful empire that controlled all of Mesopotamia and beyond.

Throughout the years of Assyrian rule, which was often harsh, the Babylonians dreamed of regaining their independence. In 612 B.C. they were finally able to make this dream come true when, aided by an Iranian people, the Medes, a local Babylonian named Nabopolassar brought Assyria to its knees and established what modern experts call the Neo-Babylonian Empire. That realm was relatively short-lived, lasting only from 626 to 539 B.C. But its vigorous, active rulers erected many new cities, palaces, and temples and took control of all of Mesopotamia. Nabopolassar's son, Nebuchadnezzar II (reigned 605–562 B.C.), constructed the famous Hanging Gardens of Babylon, later listed among the Seven Wonders of the Ancient World.

The Neo-Babylonian rulers also produced much fine art, including literature. As near as scholars can tell, most of the literary works were, as they had been in the past, tales of the exploits of the gods and mythical characters such as Gilgamesh. Several written episodes from the Babylonian creation stories have been found on tablets dating to Neo-Babylonian times.

No complete or nearly complete version of the Gilgamesh myth from this period has yet been found in the ruins of ancient Babylon. However, it is highly likely that such a document once existed. After all, the so-called standard version of that tale, on which nearly all modern retellings of the story are based, was found in the wreckage of the library of the Assyrian monarch Ashurbanipal. He reigned from 668 to 627 B.C., just prior to the founding of the Neo-Babylonian realm. Nabopolassar and Nebuchadnezzar almost certainly had their own version of Gilgamesh's story in their own library, a work that scholars hope will eventually be found.

Another myth actually involved one of the Neo-Babylonian rulers, although one whose historical reality is questionable. She was a legendary Babylonian queen named Nitocris (n'TOK-ris), who may have been Nebuchadnezzar's

Nabu the Wise

One of the more revered of the Babylonian gods was Nabu, son of the chief deity Marduk. Nabu oversaw scribes, literacy, and by extension, wisdom. To make themselves seem smarter and more respectable, several Babylonian rulers incorporated variations of his name into their own—for instance, *Nabo*nidus and *Nebu*chadnezzar.

The Anunnaki Erect Babylon

The Anunnaki appear in several Mesopotamian myths. They play a particularly important role in the Babylonian creation myth in which Marduk is the principal character. After he created humanity, he assigned some of the Anunnaki to guard the heavens and some to guard earth. As seen in this excerpt from the tale, he also ordered them to erect the city of Babylon:

The Anunnaki opened their mouths and said to Marduk, their lord: "Now, O lord, you who have caused our deliverance, what shall be our homage to you? Let us build a shrine . . . [and] let us repose in it! Let us build a throne, a recess for his abode! On the day that we arrive we shall repose in it." When Marduk heard this, [he said] "Construct Babylon, whose building you have requested, Let its brickwork be fashioned. You shall name it 'The Sanctuary.'" The Anunnaki applied the implement [got to work]; For one whole year they molded bricks. When the second year arrived, they raised high the head of Esagila [the main temple complex]. They set up in it an abode [holy shrine] for Marduk, Ellil, and Ea.

E.A. Speiser, trans. *Enuma Elish*. In *The Ancient Near East: An Anthology of Texts and Pictures*, edited by J.B. Pritchard. Princeton: Princeton University Press, 2011, p. 34.

A reconstruction of the ancient city of Babylon. In the Babylonian creation myth, Babylon's patron god, Marduk, tells the Anunnaki (gods) to build Babylon.

daughter or wife. The fifth-century-B.C. Greek historian Herodotus described her in his history book after visiting Babylon. According to Herodotus, she was responsible for many of the large-scale building projects usually credited to Nebuchadnezzar.

Herodotus also recounted a charming tale of a practical joke credited to Nitocris. In it she had the following words inscribed above the sealed entrance to her tomb: "If any king of Babylon hereafter is short of money, let him open my tomb and take as much as he likes. But this must be done only in case of need." Later the Persian monarch Darius I, whose predecessors had conquered Babylon, opened the tomb even though he did not need the money. He found the chamber empty except for the queen's body and another inscription, which read: "If you had not been insatiably greedy and eager to get money by the most despicable means, you would never have opened the tomb of the dead!"[10]

Early Religious Beliefs

Despite a few tall tales about kings, queens, and other past humans, the vast majority of Babylonian myths dealt with the gods and their relationship with humanity. So for the most part, Babylonian mythology was closely related to and dependent on religious beliefs and practices. Those fundamental aspects of religion developed over a long time, beginning thousands of years before even the Sumerians arose in the region. Indeed, the first expressions of religious belief in ancient Mesopotamia developed at some unknown point in Neolithic times—beginning between 10,000 and 9000 B.C. (11,000 to 12,000 years ago). *Neolithic* means "New Stone Age." The Neolithic era was the period in which people knew agriculture but still used stone tools and weapons. It ended in Mesopotamia in about 4000 B.C. when the residents learned to smelt metals.

Initially, the people of the region did not worship human-like gods. Rather, they prayed to invisible supernatural forces or powers called numina. These corresponded to natural phenomena and substances, including water, wind, lightning, the sky, the moon, the sun, and so forth. Besides the sun, which brought light and warmth, the most important numen was probably water, which was essential for supporting plant, animal, and human life. It appears that people believed that the numen of water, like other numina, was conscious and capable of applying itself in whatever manner it desired. Thus, water could either give life by being plentiful and pure, or

A Popular Storm God

A number of Babylonian gods were thought to control the weather. Among them was Ishkur, a storm god worshipped widely in the ancient Middle East. Also called Adad or Hadad, he was viewed by the Babylonians as a son of the major deity Ellil (the Sumerian Enlil).

it could destroy life, including humans, by being impure or by unleashing disastrous floods. Because such forces were formless, no concrete myths about them yet existed.

As time went on, however, and people in the region constructed more complex settlements and social organization, they began to see nature, including its controlling forces, in more sophisticated ways. As part of this cultural advancement, people increasingly endowed natural forces with human intelligence, motivations, and emotions. From this the next logical step was providing those forces with human form. The Sumerians and Babylonians came to picture their gods in human form principally because that shape was the most familiar one associated with intelligent thinking and actions. In other words, humans were the only known living things in the visible world that could think. So if the *in*visible natural forces could also think, it stood to reason that they, too, must be shaped like humans. Yet people readily acknowledged that those divinities were human-like only on the surface. The gods were clearly far more powerful and capable than any mere person. As Samuel N. Kramer put it:

> All human society as they knew it, all human activity, was directed by people. The universe, too, they imagined, must therefore be run by anthropomorphic, or humanlike beings, generally unperceivable [invisible] to lowly mortals. The mighty beings in charge of the universe must be more powerful and effective than their human counterparts on Earth, and these beings must live forever, for the unthinkable alternative was utter confusion at their death.[11]

The next advance in religious concepts in early Mesopotamia was to assume the human-like gods had talents, ideas, and social customs similar to those of people. Moreover, visualizing the gods this way allowed people to picture those divinities accomplishing various tasks, deeds, and adventures. Thereby, the first myths appeared. According to H.W.F. Saggs:

> A settlement had always needed the protection of supernatural powers in order to flourish, so as these powers took anthropomorphic form, every city had its own [protective] god or goddess. People now came to believe that city-states were aboriginal [the earliest] creations of their gods, and that the gods had decreed all aspects of human society from the beginning. Therefore, because within the developing city-states there were various institutions, and officials responsible for directing different functions, there must have been a corresponding pattern in the divine world. Consequently the great gods, and the deities of the cities, were thought of as having their own courts, with consorts [spouses] and families, and extensive staffs ranging from viziers [chief officials] down to hairdressers. Every human activity and craft was believed to be the responsibility of some deity.[12]

The Principal Gods

In this way a huge pantheon, or group of gods, developed among the early Sumerians. By about 2600 B.C., when Sumerian civilization was at its height and featured a complex network of hundreds of towns and cities, nearly four thousand individual gods were recognized in the Tigris-Euphrates valley. Also by that time, most of these deities had one or more myths associated with them.

The Babylonian's chief god, Marduk (MAR-dook), for example, was the subject of several myths that delineated his roles and deeds. The most important of these were his organization of the universe and his creation of human beings, both described in a colorful myth. By the time Babylonian civilization was at its height in the second and first millennia B.C., Marduk had assumed many (though certainly not all) of the roles and powers of the leader of the Sumerian gods, Enlil. The Babylonians still recognized Enlil, calling him Ellil, but to them he was a lesser deity, primarily a weather

An alabaster statue of the goddess Ishtar from the fourth century B.C. Sumerians and Babylonians chose to picture their gods in human form because that form was associated with intelligent thinking and action.

god. The demotion in importance of the older Sumerian god Enlil likely occurred gradually over a long period, during which the Babylonians invested their own, newer deity, Marduk, with increasingly higher status.

Although there were some clear differences between Enlil and Marduk, most of the Babylonian gods were fairly close or even identical equivalents of Sumerian deities. Among the more prominent were the sun god Shamash (the Sumerian Utu), the moon god Sin (Nanna), and the goddess of love and sexual passion, Ishtar (Inanna). In addition to love and sex, Ishtar oversaw war, protected rulers of dynasties, and was identified with the "evening star," the planet Venus. Ea, called Enki by the Sumerians, was another important Babylonian god. He was the deity of the waters flowing above and below the ground, and artists frequently depicted him with springs of water flowing from his shoulders or from a vase he held in his hands. Ea was also a god of wisdom and the divine patron of craftspeople.

Besides these and other major gods, the Babylonians held in awe a number of minor deities and supernatural beings. The Igigi, for instance, who may have numbered as many as three hundred or more, were sort of divine laborers who did menial jobs for the leading gods. A second group of minor gods, the Anunnaki (or Annunaki), also performed various tasks for the major deities. The Anunnaki closely resembled the angels often mentioned in the Hebrew/Christian Old Testament. This was no coincidence. A large number of Hebrews, likely including the authors of several biblical books, lived in Babylonia in the mid-first millennium B.C. They became closely familiar with local culture and religion and borrowed several Babylonian religious concepts. In the Old Testament, the angels based on the Anunnaki are referred to as the Jedi or Nephilim.

Rules to Live By

People believed that the gods had not only created humanity, but also set down rules to govern both nature and the human condition. The Babylonians called these regulations *parsu*. (The Sumerians called them *me*, pronounced MAY.) The *parsu* defined the proper conduct or workings of religious rituals, government offices, military campaigns, common professions, and arts and crafts. Two deities—Anu and Ellil—supposedly supervised the *parsu*. Moreover, the gods were not alone in their concern that humans should follow these rules. As Kramer pointed out, the *parsu* were a response to people's

> yearning for reassurance in a troubling world. They needed to believe that the universe and all its parts, once created, would continue to operate in an orderly and effective manner, not subject to disintegration and deterioration. . . . Mortal men could take comfort in the knowledge that the blue sky, the teeming earth . . . [and] the wild sea, were all acting in accordance with the rules of the gods.[13]

To emphasize the great importance of the rules, the Babylonians turned to a well-known myth in which the great Ellil himself was guilty of breaking one of them. In the era before humans were created, the story went, Ellil was out for a walk and came upon a beautiful young goddess, Ninlil, who was swimming naked in a large pool of water. The sight of her so filled him with desire that he went over and kissed her. She immediately resisted his advance, but he refused to stop. Ellil dragged Ninlil away and raped her. It did not take long for the other gods to find out what had happened, and they were extremely disturbed by it, as well as terribly disappointed with Ellil. By committing such an immoral, mean-spirited act, they told him, he had not only sinned, but also broken the very rules he himself had created to make the world and life orderly and secure. Despite his high position and authority, they said, he must be punished for his misdeed, or else the *parsu* would be meaningless. Accordingly, the other gods banished Ellil to the Underworld. The rape had caused Ninlil to become pregnant with Sin, god of the moon, so she joined Ellil in the dark depths so that when the child was born he would know both his parents.

This starkly dramatic and somber myth demonstrated to the Babylonians and other inhabitants of Mesopotamia the seriousness of keeping the *parsu* intact and unbroken. The

A Babylonian tablet describes the parsu, regulations that defined proper conduct for religious rituals, military campaigns, professions, and arts and crafts.

story made it abundantly clear that any person who committed a sin must and would be punished. After all, the very divine being who had created the rules of right conduct had been severely punished for breaking one of them. In this way religion and mythology had a direct and meaningful influence on Babylonians of all walks of life.

CHAPTER 2

Searching for the Beginnings of Things

Back in 1917, when modern studies of ancient Babylonia were still fairly young, the distinguished scholar George A. Barton wrote, "What a fascination the problem of beginnings had for the ancient Babylonians. [Surviving ancient] texts make it clear that a number of myths were cherished which professed to tell how [humanity] was formed and how the elements of civilization, as they were known in Babylonia, came into existence."[14]

Since Barton wrote those words, numerous archaeological discoveries have confirmed the Babylonian obsession with how things of all kinds began. Several of these findings relate to aspects of the New Year's festival celebrated annually in March, on the first day of spring, in Babylonia. This holiday was by far the biggest and most important in ancient Mesopotamia at the time. It lasted a full eleven days, and virtually everyone in the country, including slaves, celebrated enthusiastically. During these days people prayed, sacrificed animals to the gods, and enjoyed lavish feasts. They also constructed large, colorful images of various deities and assembled them in the Esagila, the main temple complex in the national capital, Babylon. There people from all across Babylonia took part in an enormous procession, a parade in which they solemnly carried the divine images. Chief among them was that of Marduk, prime god in the Babylonian pantheon. As one expert tells it, Marduk's decorated figure rode

on a sumptuous, jewel-bedecked chariot. Led by the king . . . this spectacular [pageant] proceeded from the Esagila, along the impressively decorated Sacred Way, through the Ishtar Gate, and out of the city to [a beautiful] shrine by the Euphrates . . . where the great event of the festival now took place—"the decreeing of the fate" of the king, symbolizing his realm, for the coming year.[15]

Another high point of the festival involved the recitation by a priest, in a loud voice before a huge crowd, of the myth of Marduk's creation of the universe and human race. The Babylonians actually had several creation myths of various lengths and content, but the one starring Marduk was the most sacred and important. The Babylonians also had myths that explained how many other aspects of nature, religion, society, and even specific tools, rocks, and other objects came to be.

Many Babylonian rituals ended in enormous processions. Here the god Marduk rides with the king in a religious procession through the Gate of Ishtar.

The Perfect Place for Creation

Among these abundant myths of beginnings were some that told how various gods, along with many new kinds of trees and other plants, originated. These stories typically envisioned one or a few primeval deities fashioning other gods and failed to explain how the initial divinities had begun. This did not bother the average Babylonian. He or she either assumed that those first gods had always been around or else figured it was not up to lowly humans to question where their creators had come from.

Among these tales of divine origins was the myth of Ea (the Sumerian Enki) and Ninhursag. Ninhursag, the so-called Lady of the Mountain, started out as an early Sumerian mother goddess who roamed the countryside and oversaw wild animals. She had a number of alternate names, including Nintu, Mamma, and Aruru. It became common for kings to take advantage of her motherly image by claiming that she loved them and approved of their rule. By Babylonian times Ninhursag had come to be identified with Damkina (or Damgalnuna), the mother of the head god, Marduk.

In her original myth she and Ea, god of freshwater and wisdom, dwelled in an extremely ancient land called Dilmun (or Tilmun). It was a sort of lush paradise—the Mesopotamian equivalent of the biblical Garden of Eden. In the beginning of the story, Dilmun is described as

> the land that knew neither sickness nor death nor old age, where the raven uttered no cry, where lions and wolves killed not, and unknown were the sorrows of widowhood or the wailing of the sick. And it was in Dilmun, at that time that [Ea], the wise god of Magic and the Sweet Waters, the Patron of Crafts and Skills, met, fell in love, and [had sex] with the Lady of the Stony Earth, Ninhursag.[16]

The reason the Babylonians pictured Dilmun as a green, lovely place in which sickness and violence did not exist is not hard to fathom. Like the Sumerians before them, they lived in an originally arid environment that had been made green in many places by cleverly diverting the waters of the

Stairways to Heaven

Among the various shrines the Baby-lonians built in honor of the gods, the largest and most imposing were the ziggurats, huge pyramid-like structures made of countless numbers of mud bricks. Unlike Egyptian pyramids, ziggurats had no internal chambers. Also, ziggurats had large stairways or ramps on one or more sides so that priests or rulers could ascend to the top, which was flat. (In compari-son, Egyptian pyramids had no stairways on the outside and came to a point at the top.) On a ziggurat's summit rested a small chapel or temple in which priests prayed and/or performed various ceremonies to honor a god or gods. In fact, ziggurats were meant to be ramps to the realm of the gods, in a sense "stairways to heav-en." These structures also had political meaning because the cities or kingdoms that built them employed them partly as propaganda to show off their wealth and power. Archaeologists have uncovered the remains of thirty-two ziggurats in and around the Mesopotamian plains to date. Only a few sections of the base survive from the Etemenanki, the great ziggurat in Babylon dedicated to the god Marduk.

A Babylonian ziggurat in modern-day Agargouf, Iraq. Ziggurats had large stairways or ramps so priests could ascend this "stairway to heaven" for religious rituals.

twin rivers and irrigating the once dry plains. The assumption was that if mere humans could manage that feat, the gods certainly could do so. In the distant past, therefore, when only a few gods populated the world, the land must have been green, fertile, and productive. Moreover, the Babylonians reasoned, humans were imperfect, which explained in part why their world featured disease, suffering, and other ills. It seemed only logical that the prehuman world must have lacked such problems. In general, to those who first authored the creation myths, a fertile, innocent world such as Dilmun seemed a perfect environment for acts of creation to occur.

Ea Learns a Lesson

According to Ea and Ninhursag's myth, that is exactly what happened. The two deities fell in love and had sexual relations, which produced a daughter, whom they named Ninsar. It took only nine days for Ninsar to become an adult. She was so beautiful that her father, Ea, became attracted to her, and before long she was pregnant. Ninsar gave birth to a daughter named Ninkurra, who also matured in a mere nine days. History now seemed to repeat itself, as Ea found himself attracted to his granddaughter and had sex with her, too, producing still another goddess, who came to be called Uttu.

At this point, Ninhursag found out what was going on and intervened. She "frowned at Ea's unbridled lust" and worked out a plan to put her husband's fertility to better use. This time it gave rise to eight new varieties of plants. The curious Ea desired to know how these trees and herbs tasted, so he ate some of them, which irritated Ninhursag. She scolded him:

> You, [Ea], came out of the blue into many maidens' lives, set yourself up like a squatter within their hearts. . . . But even then you were not satisfied in your lust to know and experience everything, so you turned to the newly created Plants World. You, [Ea], tasted each one . . . [and] always took without giving anything back. . . . For all this, you deserve a mighty lesson. . . . May the suffering you inflicted return to you threefold![17]

Ea's suffering took the form of pain he felt when he and Ninhursag made love once more. This time the experience caused eight different parts of his body to ache, and a new god was born for each of those eight pains. Satisfied that Ea had learned his lesson, Ninhursag built him a house, and once more deeply in love, they fell into each other's arms and kissed.

The Babylonians saw the theme of this myth as fertility, since numerous gods and plants sprang from the lovemaking

An artist's conception of the temptation of Ea. Ninhursag frowned on Ea's unbridled lust and worked out a plan to put her husband's fertility to better use.

of two primeval deities. Here, ultimately, the production of plants to make the earth green was of primary importance. The incidences of incest in the story may be disturbing to modern Western readers. But to the Babylonians, the idea of a god having sex with his daughter and granddaughter was acceptable when it involved acts of creation. Any concerns about social taboos in such a case were outweighed by the need to ensure that abundant crops would be there to feed and support humanity. As one scholar explains:

> Agrarian and pastoral fertility were matters of considerable concern to Mesopotamian religion. Many temples [were] praised for their role in helping produce he-gal, the fertility and prosperity of their cities; many gods [were] invoked for fertility; many kings [were] lauded for their role in the bringing of fertility. . . .

> The religious preoccupation with fertility reflects the ecology of . . . Mesopotamia, [where] surplus production resulted from irrigation. . . . [Myths about divine fertility and] rituals and prayers for fertility decreased anxiety about harvest, motivated people for agricultural labor, and enabled them to express awe and gratification at the existence of a stable agricultural surplus and the benefits it brought.[18]

The Mighty Marduk

Even more important among the Babylonian creation myths was the story of how Marduk fashioned the universe and human beings. Because it was recited each year at the New Year's festival in Babylon, it was sanctioned and promoted by the government. So people viewed it in a sense as the official version of creation.

The written epic based on this crucial myth is known as the *Enuma Elish*, a title that comes from its opening words, which translate as "when on high." It consists of about one thousand lines, gathered from a total of seven baked clay tablets found by archaeologists in assorted Babylonian and Assyrian ruins. When noted scholar George Smith published the first translation in 1876, people in the West saw resemblances between it and the creation story in the book of Genesis in the Bible. Both describe the existence of vast primeval waters, a god or gods moving over or through those waters, a deity or deities deciding to punish humans by destroying them in a great flood, and a man saving his family and many animals from the floodwaters by building a large boat. There are also a number of differences between the two.

Like Genesis, the main Babylonian creation story begins sometime in the distant past, presumably at the dawn of time. Instead of Genesis's single creator-God, however, the Babylonian version features a progression of creator-deities, each of which arises from those before it. Thus, Tiamat, who personified salt water, mated with Apsu, an early version of Ea who embodied freshwater, and from them sprang other divine forces. According to the story, "Lahmu and Lahamu were called into being," and after more time had passed, "Anshar and Kishar were created," and later still, "there came forth Anu, their son."[19]

Anu was a key deity in both the creation myth and the Mesopotamian pantheon, although he diminished in importance over time. Dutch researcher Micha F. Lindemans describes Anu:

> The ancient Sumero-Babylonian god of the firmament, the "great above," . . . is referred to as "the Father" and "King of the Gods." . . . Not only is he the father of the gods, but also of a great number of demons, whom he sends to [plague] humans. . . . Anu later retreated more and more into the background. He retires to the upper heavens and leaves the affairs of the universe to Marduk and a younger generation of gods.[20]

Anu's son, Ea, and Tiamat's consort, Apsu, played important roles in the unfolding story of creation. Apsu became increasingly annoyed at the loud chatter of the multiplying gods and decided it would be a good idea to destroy them. Ea got wind of this nefarious plot and stopped Apsu in his tracks. This act angered Tiamat, who sought to punish the upstart Ea. To this end, Tiamat spawned a horde of repellent creatures, including

> monster-serpents, sharp of tooth, and merciless of fang; with poison, instead of blood, she filled their bodies. Fierce monster-vipers she clothed with terror, with

Marduk rides his chariot to do battle with Tiamat in the Babylonian myth of creation.

splendor she decked them, she made them of lofty stature. Whoever beheld them, terror overcame him, their bodies reared up and none could withstand their attack. She set up vipers and dragons, and . . . hurricanes, and raging hounds, and scorpion-men, and mighty tempests, and fish-men, and rams. They bore cruel weapons, without fear of the fight.[21]

Leading this awful assemblage was the hideous beast Kingu. He was given charge of the Tablet of Destinies, which foretold the future fates of the gods and humans. Soon Ea discovered what Tiamat was up to but realized that he was not strong enough to resist the monsters alone. So he called forth his own son, the fearless and forceful Marduk. Those deities who decided to take Ea's side in the coming fight gave Marduk supreme authority. Donning his armor, Marduk ran out onto the battlefield, and the very sight of him filled Tiamat, Kingu, and their murderous minions with sheer terror. In the conflict that followed, the mighty Marduk attacked and slew Tiamat, then took the Tablet of Destinies away from the defeated Kingu.

A Number of Truths

Having thus triumphed over evil, Marduk proceeded to create the universe. First, he sliced Tiamat's lifeless body in half and used the top half to fashion the sky. Then he created the moon's phases, showered the sky with stars, and started the progression of the seasons. Finally, he created human beings, whom he fashioned from clay, but needing fluids to animate the dirt, he killed Kingu and used that creature's blood for this purpose. "I will create man who shall inhabit the Earth," Marduk declared, "that the service of the gods may be established, and that their shrines may be built."[22] Thoroughly impressed, the other gods bowed down to Marduk and sang his praises. They also erected the great temple compound in Babylon known as the Esagila, which humans would employ as their central location for worshipping the gods.

The Babylonians and other Mesopotamians recognized what they believed were a number of momentous and fundamental truths in this myth. First, they had been created by a beneficent god who had decisively defeated evil. That made humans, via their intimate connection with their heavenly father Marduk, essentially good.

Second, Marduk's decree that people would be in the gods' service indicated that humans were expected to be submissive to, or slaves of, those deities. After all, men and women had been formed from clay, the most abundant, basest, cheapest, and least remarkable material on the Mesopotamian plains. As a

The Giant in the Forest

The monster, sometimes referred to as a giant, that Gilgamesh slew when visiting the distant forest is called Huwawa (or Humbaba) in the original text. Supposedly the creature guarded wooded foothills of the Cedar Mountain, situated to the west of the Tigris-Euphrates valley.

result, the Babylonians believed that they were equally base by nature. Also, their servile status implied that they lacked free will. "Convinced that they were created to be slaves and servants of the gods," Samuel N. Kramer pointed out, they meekly "accepted the divine decisions, even the inexplicable and seemingly unjustified ones. . . . A [Babylonian] who, like the biblical Job, was burdened with undeserved troubles, was taught [from birth] not to argue and complain in the face of

Marduk slew Tiamat and cut her body in half to create the sky, moon phases, and the progressions of the seasons. He then created humans from clay.

inscrutable [unexplained] misfortune, but to admit that he was, inevitably, a depraved soul."[23]

In addition, Marduk's creation myth explained how the first temples and other shrines to the gods, in particular the most revered ones, came to be in Babylon. The Babylonians of the first millennium B.C. were well aware that their recent ancestors had built the existing Esagila. But the creation myth informed them that the original temple complex that had once stood on that same spot had been put there by the gods themselves.

Cuneiform Symbols

When the Sumerians developed their main writing system, the symbols carved or pressed into wet clay looked like little wedges, which were arranged in various, sometimes complex, patterns. Modern scholars dubbed these symbols "cuneiform," after the Latin word *cuneus*, meaning "wedge- or nail-shaped."

The Invention of Writing and Taming of Nature

Whereas myths like that of Marduk's creation of humans presented largely fanciful descriptions of how things began, others captured memories of some real beginnings. One of the many tales associated with the hero Gilgamesh is an example of this. In it he visited a large, deep forest, where he slew a monster and then spent time chopping down trees and digging up their stumps. Many experts think this story reflects a time, perhaps in the late 3000s or early 2000s B.C., when the residents of the Mesopotamian plains exploited and extensively cut back the few forests that still existed in the region.

Similarly, it is thought that another myth recalls the invention of writing messages on tablets. The story told in the epic titled *Enmerkar and the Lord of Aratta* is set in "those days of yore" before "commerce was practiced."[24] At the time, the myth recounts, Enmerkar, king of one of the first cities, Uruk, was engaged in a war of threats with the ruler of the faraway land of Aratta. (Aratta's location is unclear, but it may have been in what is now southern Armenia or southeastern Turkey.)

At first, the words exchanged between these monarchs were conveyed in the original preliteracy manner—by having a

Diplomatic correspondence in cuneiform on a clay tablet. Cuneiform writing was believed to have originated with correspondence between Enmerkar, king of Uruk, and the ruler of a land called Aratta.

messenger memorize and deliver them in person. But eventually the messages became so lengthy that the poor fellow could no longer keep all the details straight. According to the surviving portions of the epic, the messenger's "mouth was tired," meaning that his memory had been taxed so badly that nothing was coming out his mouth! So the apparently clever "lord of [Uruk] patted some clay and wrote the message as if on a tablet. Formerly, the writing of messages on clay was not established. Now, under that sun and on that day, it was indeed so. The lord of [Uruk] inscribed the message like a tablet."[25]

In a similar manner, some other myths seem to carry the germs of early technological discoveries and breakthroughs. The tale of *Ninurta and Agog*, for instance, recalls how the early inhabitants of Mesopotamia learned to counteract natural landslides and to use the various rocks and minerals in the mountains lying to the north to aid civilized life on the plains. Appropriately, the chief character, Ninurta, was a deity of irrigation and nature before he became a major war god.

One day, the story goes, Ninurta heard that the rocks in the hills had rebelled against the gods and were rolling down onto the plains in an attempt to wreck the towns there. Someone warned Ninurta that the chief rock warrior, Agog (or Asag), was extremely formidable and could not be stopped by ordinary means. Ninurta hurried to the foothills. There he tried smashing Agog with his hammer, but to no avail. Finally, Ninurta managed to vanquish the monster and

The Exalted Pickax

The beginning, or invention, of one of the chief tools used in ancient Babylonia—the pickax—was credited to the Sumerian god Enlil (the Babylonian Ellil). It was not only essential to agriculture but was also the implement with which Enlil created human beings (a task later said to have been accomplished by Marduk). According to a surviving tablet:

So that the earth could grow humankind, [Enlil/Marduk] created the pickax. . . . Stretching out his arm straight toward the pickax and the basket, [that god] sang the praises of his pickaxe. He drove his pickax into the earth. In the hole which he had made was humankind. While the people of the land were breaking through the ground, he eyed [them] in steadfast fashion. The pickax and the basket [made it possible for people to] build cities. . . . The steadfast house [the pickax] causes to prosper. . . . The pickax, its fate is decreed by father Enlil. The pickax is exalted.

Quoted in W.L. Moran, ed. *Toward the Image of Tammuz and Other Essays on Mesopotamian History and Culture.* Cambridge, MA: Harvard University Press, 1970, pp. 113–114.

his rock soldiers by learning to build earthen embankments that channeled falling stones and mountain streams safely onto the plains.

Ninurta then either rewarded or punished the different rocks and minerals, depending on which ones had opposed him or helped him in the battle. One of the kinds of stone that he rewarded was diorite, one of the hardest and most useful minerals known to the Babylonians and other early peoples (in part because a diorite hammer can crack or crush most other kinds of stone). "You did not attack me," Ninurta told the diorite. Therefore, people "shall extract you from the highland countries" and "bring you" to the plains, where "you shall shape Strong Copper like leather and then you shall be perfectly adapted for my heroic arm." And a sample of diorite "shall be placed in . . . my temple."[26]

This tale was extremely ancient and, based on what historians know of the technical accomplishments of Babylonia, must have predated Babylonian times by at least a millennium or more. But the Babylonians still knew it, along with Ninurta's other myths. These and other stories like them reflected the particular materials and customs that were most common in the region. This provided people with information about their world and their lives that gave them peace of mind and also educated them (in a crude way by today's standards) about both nature and their past.

CHAPTER 3

Quests for the Secrets of Immortality

The most famous and popular Babylonian myths, both in ancient times and later ages, were those dealing with the hero Gilgamesh. According to the Sumerian King Lists, he was a real ruler of the city of Uruk in the early third millennium B.C. If those lists are right and he *was* a historical person, his actual deeds are now a mystery. What have survived are several tall tales about him that are sometimes told separately and other times combined into one long story most often called the *Epic of Gilgamesh*.

The overriding theme of that epic is the title character's quest for the secret of eternal life. Other surviving Mesopotamian myths also deal with heroes who searched for a way of gaining immortality, suggesting that the people of Mesopotamia found the idea of living forever quite compelling. As for why they would feel this way, some scholars think it had something to do with prevailing views of the afterlife. Unlike a number of other ancient peoples, including the Hebrews and Greeks, the Babylonians believed there was little or nothing to look forward to following death. So perhaps this bred a fascination for finding a way to circumvent it. The general belief that the gods were immortal and knew the secret of prolonging life suggested that eternal life was possible, if only humans could find the secret.

The most famous Babylonian myth is the Epic of Gilgamesh. *This statue from the palace of Sargon depicts Gilgamesh taming a lion.*

Another reason the Babylonians and other Mesopotamians found the notion of eternal life captivating may have been that the Tigris-Euphrates valley was prone to sudden disasters, which could make life seem especially short and precarious. As one scholar puts it, the twin rivers were unpredictable and "could lay a district waste for a generation in one spring flood. [Also, Mesopotamia] bordered the desert with its dust storms . . . locust swarms, and raiding Bedouin [nomadic Arab tribes]. Thus the drama . . . of Mesopotamian mythology expresses the essentially emotional relationship of man to his environment in . . . both its natural and supernatural aspect."[27]

Gilgamesh Travels West

Whatever the reasons for the Babylonians' keen interest in Gilgamesh's hunt for immortality, his quest began shortly after he suffered a personal tragedy. A few years before, he had been a selfish, thoughtless, and unpopular ruler. So to help the people of Uruk, the gods arranged for Gilgamesh to discover and take in Enkidu, a hairy, uncouth character living with the beasts in the countryside. While trying to tame the wild man, Gilgamesh became friends with him. Just as the gods had intended, Enkidu turned out to be kinder and more responsible than the king and was a positive influence that turned Gilgamesh into a model ruler.

Gilgamesh and Enkidu became inseparable and had several adventures together. But eventually, Ishtar, the goddess of love, intervened. She desired to make Gilgamesh her lover, but he refused, and in retaliation she cast a deadly curse on Enkidu that caused him to fall ill and die. Heartbroken at the loss of his best friend, Gilgamesh wept openly and asked all aspects of nature to grieve with him. He said:

> May every wild beast mourn for Enkidu. . . . May the mountain, the hill, the valley, the very fertile earth mourn for Enkidu. May the trees, and the grass and moss on every rock mourn for Enkidu. May the water in the sea, in the lake, in the rivers, in the dew mourn for Enkidu. May old men, may young men . . . , may children and women of every kind mourn for Enkidu. . . . I weep and I mourn for Enkidu. Enkidu was my friend.[28]

Gilgamesh had never experienced such a deeply emotional loss before, so he wandered alone across the plains for several weeks, contemplating the nature of death. He tried to come to grips with, understand, and accept the inevitability and finality of death. But he could not bring himself to accept that people must one day die and be snuffed out of existence. He decided that the secret of immortality must exist somewhere and that he must find it in order to spare himself and his fellow humans the horrors of death.

Gilgamesh had heard rumors that a very old man named Utnapishtim, the former king of the city of Shuruppak, knew where to find the secret of eternal life. The problem was that Utnapishtim lived on an island in the mysterious great sea situated far to the west of Mesopotamia. So it would be a long, arduous, and no doubt dangerous journey.

But Gilgamesh was determined to succeed in his quest. After weeks of traveling overland, he reached a beautiful

Gilgamesh and Enkidu had several adventures together, including the slaying of the bull of Ishtar (depicted here).

garden lying along the coast of the great sea. The garden was tended by a goddess named Siduri, who told the visitor that he should turn around and go back to Uruk. "No man walks on the deadly night sea as [the god] Shamash does," she warned. "Shamash is the only one who can. When a mortal takes a step, quick he sinks, and just as quick comes death. . . . O Mighty King, remember now that only gods stay in eternal watch. Humans come then go, that is the way fate decreed on the Tablets of Destiny."[29]

These words did not faze Gilgamesh, however. He insisted that Siduri take him to Utnapishtim's boatman, which she did. The traveler then persuaded the boatman to carry him to Utnapishtim's island, a journey that took a month.

Gilgamesh the Wrestler

Like male friends in all ages, Gilgamesh and Enkidu bonded partly through a shared love of sports. As a young man, Gilgamesh was a champion wrestler, and early in the *Epic of Gilgamesh*, the two characters become involved in a street brawl that ends up testing their wrestling skills.

Memories of Ancient Traders?

The Babylonians and other Mesopotamians who read or heard Gilgamesh's story were aware of the existence of the great western sea, now called the Mediterranean. But to them it was indeed a mysterious place far outside their civilized sphere, which was dominated by the Tigris and Euphrates Rivers and Persian Gulf. The section of the myth in which Gilgamesh journeyed to an island in that sea seems to derive from an early era when Sumerian travelers, probably merchants, first encountered the Mediterranean. The Sumerians soon developed thriving trade routes stretching as far away as India in the east and Egypt and Anatolia in the west. Subsequently, when Sumerian civilization waned, the Babylonians took over most of these trade routes.

Siduri's garden and the boatman who ferried Gilgamesh to the island likely reflect memories of the early peoples who lived in Palestine on the eastern Mediterranean coast. Those shores enjoyed a warm climate and abundant rainfall, so they would have seemed garden-like to Sumerian and later Babylonian traders coming out of the more arid plains.

An Agonizing Speech

According to the surviving text of Gilgamesh's quest for immortality, when he reached the Mediterranean coast and approached the boatman, the latter said, "Your face is clenched with grief's tight grip and dead seems where you're at. You act as if you had no home except wilderness terribly born."[1] In reply, Gilgamesh gave these heartfelt, agonizing words, which anyone in any age who has lost a loved one can readily understand:

True it be [that] my face is clenched with grief's tight grip, and surely I be better dead than feel as I do now. But ... this [is] not [a] random walk but [rather a serious] quest [inspired by] my mourning grief. Enkidu, my loyal friend. . . . It is for him whom I grieve.

Enkidu my friend for ever more will I remember [how] we strove two together to prevail over highest mountain and deepest valley in order to both serve and defy the gods above. . . . Then he died, and left me [to] weep, fit only to weep over his rotting corpse. . . . I roam alone with only his memory by my side. For Enkidu now I must roam, never stopping my weary steps. If I stop my roaming, then my heart, half gone [already], will stop. Over many seas and across many mountains I roam. I can't stop pacing. I can't stop crying.[2]

1. Maureen G. Kovacs, John Maier, and John Gardner, trans. *Epic of Gilgamesh. Tablet 8.* MythHome. www.mythome. org/Gilgamesh.html.

2. Kovacs, Maier, Gardner. *Epic of Gilgamesh. Tablet 8.*

Upon reaching the Mediterranean coast, Gilgamesh, shown right, meets with a boatman and tells him of his grief for his lost friend, Enkidu.

Having reached the coast, some of those merchants wanted to go farther—to southern Anatolia, for instance. If so, just as Gilgamesh had, they often enlisted the services of locals who had ships and knew the nearby waters. Archaeologists have determined that the Palestinian coastal town of Gebeil, later the Phoenician city of Byblos, was inhabited and thriving during the mid- to late 2000s B.C., the period when the myth of Gilgamesh's westward journey was likely first generated. It is possible that this or a similar nearby coastal town was the home of the boatman in the myth.

As for the island where the boatman took Gilgamesh in the story, there are two strong candidates. One is the large isle of Cyprus, lying directly south of Anatolia. Cyprus was heavily forested before the first millennium B.C., and it is possible that the island supplied wood to Mesopotamian traders. It has already been established that another of Gilgamesh's tales—in which he killed a monster and uprooted trees in a forest—reflects deforestation in the ancient Middle East. So the myth in which Gilgamesh sailed westward on a quest may be a distant memory of Sumerian merchants seeking new sources of timber. As noted University of California scholar Richard Cowen points out:

> It's clear that the geography and climate of southern Mesopotamia would not provide the wood fuel to support a Bronze Age civilization that worked metal, built large cities, and constructed canals and ceremonial centers that used wood, plaster, and bricks. Most timber would have to be imported from the surrounding mountains, and deforestation there, in a climate that receives occasional torrential storms, would have led to severe erosion and run-off.[30]

The other possibility is that the island in the myth was not an island at all, but actually the southern coast of Anatolia. In the 1980s archaeologists discovered that the Taurus Mountains,

The Cedars of Lebanon

The forest in which Gilgamesh kills a monster and fells a number of trees was dominated by cedar trees. It is clear that this aspect of the myth was inspired by the region now occupied by the small country of Lebanon, on the eastern Mediterranean coast, because in ancient times it was covered by dense cedar forests.

lying just north of those shores, were the major source of tin for bronze-making in the ancient Middle East. So Gilgamesh's western journey might well reflect the exploits of Sumerian and Babylonian tin traders sailing northwestward into the Mediterranean from the Palestinian coast.

No Rewards After Death

Wherever the island may really have been, when Gilgamesh reached it in the story, he met the aged Utnapishtim. The old man admitted that he indeed had received the gift of immortality from the gods. However, it had been a special gift from those deities, and it was not possible for all people to obtain eternal life.

Yet Gilgamesh was adamant about finding the secret, and Utnapishtim finally relented and revealed its location—at the bottom of the sea. The daring traveler wasted no time. He jumped into the water and brought up the magical flower containing a drug that made anyone who ate it live forever.

Thanking Utnapishtim, Gilgamesh departed for home. He was almost there when a great misfortune occurred. Gilgamesh stopped to bathe in a stream and put the plant down. At that moment, according to the myth, "a nearby serpent smelled [it] and straight to it did it go. The serpent stole and ate it, and thusly does the snake [shed and grow back its] skin once every full moon."[31]

Gilgamesh attempted to find the snake but never could, so his great quest had failed. Yet the king of Uruk had learned an important lesson: that only the gods are immortal, while humans are fated to die in the end.

This underlying theme of Gilgamesh's primary myth— that humans have nothing to look forward to after death— clearly reflected Babylonian beliefs about the afterlife. They did envision an underworld, a place where human souls might go after death. But there, they assumed, they would be condemned to live in a dull, monotonous, uninviting landscape in which they would simply exist, feeling neither happiness nor pain. As the eminent scholar of ancient Mesopotamia Gwendolyn Leick puts it:

Babylonian views on death can be gleaned from some of the literary works and from their mortuary practices. . . .

[They] did not believe in either retributions or rewards for one's [earthly] behavior after death. Instead, they were more inclined to interpret misfortune, illness, and of course death itself as a form of punishment for "sin."

Desperate for Children

The quest for immortality took a different twist in another Babylonian myth—the story of Etana. In this case the hero, a Sumerian king, was not looking for eternal life for himself, but rather in a more practical way for his progeny—essentially his family line. More specifically, he did not want to be king unless he could supply a son to carry on his family and his policies after his death. So Etana prayed to the sun god, Shamash, and asked for a son. The god told Etana to find an eagle that had lost its ability to fly because a snake had badly injured its wings, and after a long search the man located the eagle resting at the bottom of a pit. Etana carefully mended the creature's broken wings. When the great bird was once more able to fly, it carried its rescuer up into the sky. There Etana hoped to find Ishtar, the goddess of sexual passion, who it was said owned a special plant that could render a person capable of having many children. The conclusion of this tale did not survive. But according to the Sumerian King Lists, Etana did have a son who succeeded him on the throne. So the myth is likely to have ended with Etana meeting with Ishtar and her granting him access to the magical plant.

A tablet telling the tale of Etana, who looked for immortality for his children but not himself.

They grieved for the dead, lamenting their passing as Gilgamesh does in the Epic when Enkidu dies. But they accepted death as "the fate of mankind." They preferred to bury the deceased within the family compound, below the thick mud brick walls or beneath the floor of a little-used room, sometimes in clay coffins, with few if any grave-goods.[32]

Adapa's Tale

This bleak view of the afterlife explains why as children most Babylonians were routinely taught that they should make the best of their earthly lives. There was a general conception that people should make the most of the short time the gods had granted them on earth. This partly clarifies not only the long perpetuation of the tale of Gilgamesh's fruitless search for immortality, but also the appearance of this same theme in other myths. Of these, the best known was the story *Adapa*.

The mythical Adapa was a priest of the god Ea in the city of Eridu, located a few miles southeast of Uruk. Among Adapa's duties was to keep the temple well stocked with food, so he sailed his small boat out into the Persian Gulf with the intention of catching some fish. Less than an hour after departing, the man noticed dark clouds approaching. Realizing a bad storm was on the way, he headed for shore, but the tempest caught up with him and capsized the boat. At this, Adapa cursed loudly, directing his words against the god of the south wind.

Father of the Gods

Anu, whom the Sumerians called An, was one of the oldest of the Mesopotamian gods. Seen as a sort of father figure for the other gods, he was worshipped all over the region, but especially in Uruk (the biblical Erech), which was the center of his cult.

When the god Anu learned of this insult aimed at one of his own kind, he told Ea, the deity worshipped in the temple where the priest worked, to bring Adapa to him for punishment. While Ea and Adapa were en route to Anu's palace, they chatted. Adapa said that during the upcoming meeting he hoped to persuade Anu to reveal the secret of eternal life. That way Adapa would help his fellow humans immensely.

Ea, who had watched Adapa at work in the temple for a long time, took pity on him and offered to help. Adapa should greatly flatter Dumuzi and Gizzida, the minor gods who guarded the door to the throne room, Ea instructed. They would then urge Anu to be merciful with Adapa. However, Ea added, Anu would likely offer the man something to eat and drink. "When you stand before Anu," Ea said, he "will hold out for you bread of death, so you must not eat." Also, he "will hold out for you water of death, so you must not drink."[33]

Adapa followed Ea's instructions and praised Dumuzi and Gizzida. Sure enough, they then convinced Anu to forgive Adapa for cursing the god of the south wind. Next, Ea proved right again as Anu offered Adapa some food and drink. "Fetch him the bread of eternal life and let him eat!" Anu ordered his attendants. But when they brought Adapa the bread, he refused to eat it. He also would not drink the

As part of his duties, Adapa kept the temple stocked with food by fishing from his small boat, similar to the one shown here. When he was shipwrecked, he cursed one of the gods and thereby incurred their wrath.

Keeping Man in His Place?

The myth of Adapa has been interpreted in several different ways by modern experts. Here researcher Joshua J. Mark explains his view that the tale, like that of Adam and Eve in the Bible, is mainly about the "fall of man" because it "explains why human beings are mortal." The deity of wisdom, Ea, gives Adapa "great intelligence" Mark writes, but not eternal life,

And when immortality is offered Adapa by the great god Anu, Ea tricks Adapa into refusing the gift.

Though it is not expressed directly in the myth, Ea's reasoning in this seems similar to [God's] in the Genesis story from the Bible where, after Adam and Eve are cursed for eating of the Tree of the Knowledge of Good and Evil, [God] casts them out before they can also eat of the Tree of Life:

"Behold, the man is become as one of us, to know good and evil; and now, lest he put forth his hand and take also of the tree of life, and eat, and live forever; Therefore the Lord God sent him forth from the garden of Eden" (Genesis 3:22–23).

If Adam and Eve were immortal they would be on par with [God] and there would be a loss of status for [God]; and this is Ea's same reasoning in the Adapa myth. In the Genesis myth, man takes knowledge for himself by eating of the tree; in the Mesopotamian myth, the god Ea grants man knowledge in the process of creation. Knowing that Adapa is already wise, Ea (like [God] in the later story from Genesis) needs to keep man in his place.

Joshua J. Mark. "The Myth of Adapa." Ancient History Encyclopedia. February 23, 2011. www.ancient.eu/article/216.

liquid that Anu claimed was "the water of eternal life." The surprised Anu exclaimed, "Come, Adapa, why didn't you eat? Why didn't you drink? Didn't you want to be immortal?"[34]

Thinking that Anu had lied about the refreshments, Adapa once more refused to touch them. A few minutes later he thanked Anu for showing him mercy and returned to Babylonia. Anu smiled because he knew the true nature of the bread and water. Only later did Adapa learn the truth—that those substances really were the elixirs of immortality. Had Adapa consumed them, he would have enjoyed eternal life.

The Rules of Hospitality

On the surface Adapa's myth seems to make the same point that Gilgamesh's story does—namely that humans are not meant to possess eternal life. Although most ancient Babylonians likely read just that meaning into it, modern experts look at it differently. Most scholars think that the myth is a distorted recollection of the proper rules of hospitality in Mesopotamia's distant past, well before Babylonian times and maybe even before the Sumerians arose. All civilizations develop their distinctive rules of showing strangers and/or neighbors hospitality, that is, treatment to make them feel welcome. Usually that treatment includes offers of food and drink.

In this view, Anu made sure that Adapa received acceptable offers of hospitality. What made the situation different was that Anu and Ea were gods, whereas Adapa was a mere human. Anu was accustomed to entertaining fellow deities, not humans, so the food he offered Adapa was "god food," not human food. There is an underlying assumption that a person who partakes of the food of the gods can or might become a god himself, or at least immortal like those deities. Over time, this fact must have transformed the story from a parable about proper treatment of guests into a tale about a man seeking but failing to find the secret of eternal life.

Transformed in this manner, however, the story could not logically end with Adapa, who in his meeting with Anu represented all of humanity, gaining immortality. As every ancient Babylonian knew, people were very mortal. So they had never been granted eternal life. To acknowledge this reality, the storytellers were obliged to create a situation in which Adapa had been duly offered hospitality by the gods but also had not received from those deities the great secret of immortality. The only plausible way to manage this was to have one or more gods trick Adapa into turning down the offer of the miraculous food. In the words of scholar Mario Liverani:

> If Adapa had eaten and drunk, he would have become the guest who ate with the immortal gods: he would have become immortal too, because the gods—like men—could not permit someone to whom they had given bread and water to die. Adapa . . . is not punished, but he does not receive the gift of immortality. Anu is relieved [as shown by his smile] for not having been obliged by the strict rules of hospitality to change the mortal fate of humankind.[35]

A reconstruction depicts the city of Eridu in 3000 B.C. The Temple of Anu is in the foreground.

This shows how the content of ancient myths could change considerably over time, particularly in the ages

before they were committed to writing. Oral versions of myths were subject to alteration based on changing social or political situations, loss of knowledge about people and places, or even nothing more than the whims of individual storytellers. Hence, a tale that originally explained the rules of proper hospitality that had been laid down by the gods steadily morphed into one in which the gods offered a guest in their home food that could make him immortal. Similarly, the story of a Sumerian king who opened new trade routes to acquire supplies of wood and/or tin emerged many centuries later as the myth of a hero on a quest for the secret of eternal life.

In both cases, moreover, the changing content of these stories was colored by the emotional needs of both tellers and listeners. Like people in every place and time, they needed to imagine that there was more to human existence than the few years of struggle between birth and death. Myths like those of Gilgamesh and Adapa help to fulfill that need.

CHAPTER 4

The Inevitability of Conflict and Calamity

E very society and civilization in history has had to come to grips with the darker aspects of life. Sooner or later they had to face the reality that political and social strife, wars, and natural disasters are unavoidable facets of the human experience. In ancient times, myths involving these themes were common. Peoples and cultures worked out the frustrations they felt about these issues through the frequent repetition of such tales, and the Babylonians were no exception.

The Naked Goddess

Of the various forms of strife, the family kind—between husbands and wives, parents and children, or brothers and sisters—was among the more universal and familiar. So it is not surprising that one of the most famous and often-told of all Babylonian myths, *The Descent of Ishtar*, involved sibling rivalry. As in numerous other myths, the main characters were gods, whose relationships and problems symbolized those of humans.

In this case, as the title indicates, the leading character was the love goddess Ishtar, whom the Sumerians had called Inanna. Ishtar's rival was her sister Ereshkigal, queen of the dark Underworld, frequently referred to as the Land of No Return in ancient Mesopotamia. It earned this name because it was thought that once someone—whether human or god—entered that nether realm, he or she could never again return to earth's surface. It was well known that the two divine sisters did not get along. In part this was because the unhappy, ill-tempered Ereshkigal was extremely jealous of the beautiful, widely popular Ishtar.

At the beginning of the story, Ishtar decided to descend into the Underworld and pay her sister a visit. The reason for this journey was never stated in written versions of the

This Babylonian clay plaque may depict Ishtar or Ishtar's devious sister, Ereshkigal.

The Baby Snatcher

Ereshkigal was not the only mythi-cal Babylonian character associated with evil. There were all manner of demons and monsters as well. Among these, one of the most terrifying was Lamashtu, a female demon who snatched unborn children from their mothers' wombs. Not surprisingly, incidents of crib death in Babylonia were attributed to Lamashtu.

tale. Some scholars, including Samuel N. Kramer, have speculated that Ishtar was ambitious enough to want to seize her sister's subterranean kingdom. If so, the supposedly friendly trip was really a fact-finding mission in preparation for the takeover.

Whatever Ishtar's motive was, she seemed to sense that the visit might not end well. Prior to leaving, the late English scholar S.H. Hooke explained, she "instructed her vizier, Ninshubar, that if she did not return in three days he was to perform mourning rites for her, and to go in turn to the three high gods, Ellil of Nippur, Sin the moon-god of Ur, and Ea, the Babylonian god of wisdom, in Eridu, and entreat them to intervene on her behalf that she may not be put to death in the nether world."[36]

When Ishtar arrived at the gates of the Underworld, her sister sent word that she was welcome as long as she removed all of her clothes. Ishtar followed this instruction, but it turned out to be a trick. Now that Ishtar was completely naked, her body was more vulnerable to attack, and her sister took immediate advantage. Ereshkigal ordered that Ishtar be killed and that her body be hung on a hook.

Striking a Deal

Ishtar's death had huge repercussions for humans and animals. Under normal conditions, her spirit motivated sexual relations, so when she died all sexual activity in the world suddenly ceased. As the text of the written version says, "After Lady Ishtar had descended to the nether world, the bull springs not upon the cow, the ass impregnates not the jenny [female donkey], [and] in the street the man impregnates not the maiden. The man lies in his own chamber, [while] the maiden lies on her side."[37]

Moreover, Ishtar's backup plan now went into effect. Her assistant, Ninshubar, hurried to the other gods, as she had instructed him to, and ended up getting the help of the powerful deity Ea. The god hastily created two beings whose sole reason for existing was to rescue Ishtar. When they arrived in Ereshkigal's realm, they deceived her into releasing Ishtar's body to them. Then, employing the food and drink of divine immortality, they brought her back to life, which caused reproduction instantly to resume all across earth's surface.

Upon entering the Underworld, Ishtar was tricked by Ereshkigal into removing her clothes, which made her vulnerable to attack. Then Ereshkigal ordered her sister to be killed.

The love goddess's troubles were not yet over, however. There was only one way for her to leave the Underworld permanently; namely, to find a substitute to live there in her place. So, guarded by some of Ereshkigal's demons, Ishtar went to the surface to find such a replacement. It ended up being her mate, Tammuz (the Sumerian Dumuzi). Tammuz's sister, the minor goddess Geshtinanna, tried to rescue him, but to no avail. Thereafter the major parties involved negotiated a deal that called for Tammuz and his sister to alternate residence in the dark depths. Stephen Bertman remarks that they reached an agreement "by which each

A Greek Version of Ishtar's Myth?

A number of modern scholars have pointed out some close parallels between the story of Ishtar's descent into the Underworld and the ancient Greek myth of Demeter, goddess of grain crops, and her daughter Persephone. Hades, the Greek deity of the Underworld, kidnapped Persephone and took her to his subterranean kingdom. When the young woman went missing, Demeter searched for her high and low until she learned about the abduction. Then the enraged goddess allowed famine and drought to run riot across earth's surface. Zeus, king of the Greek gods, was concerned that Demeter's tantrum might destroy human civilization. So he and some other divinities reasoned with her, and they struck a deal. Hades allowed Perse-

phone to spend half of each year on earth with her mother, but she was obliged to spend the other half with him in his dark realm. Although some differences exist between the two myths, it is clear that the older Mesopotamian one strongly influenced the later Greek one. This may have come about through cultural interactions among long-distance traders from the two civilizations.

A Greek painting depicts Persephone and Hades. It is thought that the Greek myth is based on the older tale of Ishtar and Ereshkigal.

would in turn spend only half a year in the realm of the dead."[38]

Like the Sumerians before them, the Babylonians were quite clear about the meanings of this major myth. On the one hand, it was a story about familial hatreds and strife. The mean-spirited and at times brutal relationship between Ishtar and her sister demonstrated that sibling rivalry was unconstructive and potentially harmful.

More importantly, however, the tale established why humans could be confident that the steady progression of the seasons, and especially the growing period of crops in late spring and summer, would continue unabated. Crop failures and the mass starvation connected with them periodically ravaged ancient lands, including Babylonia. So worries about such losses of fertility were ever present in people's thoughts. In addition to overseeing love, Ishtar was, in her role as motivator of sexual relations, a powerful fertility deity. As god of pastures and flocks, Tammuz was also a promoter of fertility. If either one of them was stuck forever in the Underworld, disaster would surely ensue for both people and animals. The deal the gods struck, by which Ishtar was freed and Tammuz spent only half of each year in Ereshkigal's underground kingdom, ensured that life on earth's surface would continue.

Erra's Fury

Discord between siblings is by its nature a small-scale sort of conflict. Strife on a much larger scale—armed warfare—was also extremely common in ancient Mesopotamia. In Sumerian times the city-states of Sumer—among them Uruk, Ur, Nippur, Lagash, and Larsa—squabbled with one another almost incessantly. Later, in the second and first millennia B.C., the Babylonians and Assyrians were archenemies who engaged in frequent wars with each other and third-party neighbors.

One of the major Babylonian myths describing the destructive effects associated with warfare is known as *The Wrath of Erra*. (Other common names for it are *Erra and Ishum* and *The Erra Epic*.) Erra, whom the Sumerians called Nergal, was a formidable war god. The other main characters in the story are Ishum, god of fire, who also acts as Erra's faithful assistant, and Marduk, chief deity of the Babylonian pantheon.

The myth started out by describing Erra's boredom. He had not waged any wars for several years, and because he loved to fight, he longed to return to the battlefield. After deciding it was time to act, he set his sights on destroying the great city of Babylon, which he was sure would satisfy his aggressive urges.

As Erra was donning his armor, however, Ishum approached him and asked, "O Lord Erra, why have you plotted evil against the gods?" In Ishum's view, it was ill-advised "to lay waste the lands and decimate the people."[39] But Erra's mind was made up. "I am the wild bull in heaven!" he shouted. "I am the lion on Earth [and] the fiercest among the gods!" He added, "I will make Marduk angry, stir him from his dwelling, and lay waste [his] people!"[40]

When Erra approached his target, Babylon, he saw Marduk preparing to defend the city. The war god then proceeded to trick Marduk (who appears unusually dense in this particular myth) by saying that his outfit was ratty. Instantly concerned about his appearance rather than the city, Marduk left the scene to go shopping for new clothes! Not surprisingly, as soon as Marduk had disappeared from view, Erra launched his attack on Babylon. Ishum attempted to stop the massacre but was unable to prevent his boss from flattening buildings and slaying untold numbers of people.

Finally, Erra grew weary and ended his rampage. When some other gods asked him why he had destroyed Babylon, he casually answered that violence was simply central to his nature. The wise Ishum then pointed out that all was not lost. The magnificent Babylon would one day rise again.

A Rough Historical Sketch

On the surface, the tale of Erra's destruction of Babylon seems like a commentary on the horrors of war. "War is hell," as the age-old adage goes. Also, the myth reminded the Babylonians that human cities and societies are temporary, fleeting, and certain eventually to decline when the gods will it.

Yet looking at the tale from a modern vantage point, it also appears to be a somewhat garbled memory of a series of real historical events. It is important to repeat that the Babylonians and other peoples of their day did not have a clear, documented concept of their own past, sometimes even of recent events as well as distant ones. Instead, decisive happenings were remembered orally, by telling and retelling them as stories, which naturally changed, a little or a lot, over time. So after the passage of three, four, or more generations, recollections of the crucial events of a given decade or century frequently became exaggerated, mangled, and/or mixed with less historical, more fantastic elements.

This is what modern experts think happened in the case of the myth of Erra's temper tantrum. The tale was well established by the time that Neo-Babylonia rose to prominence in

Erra destroyed Babylon because he was bored and wanted to start a war.

A small stone carving records the restoration of the walls and temples of Babylon by Esarhaddon.

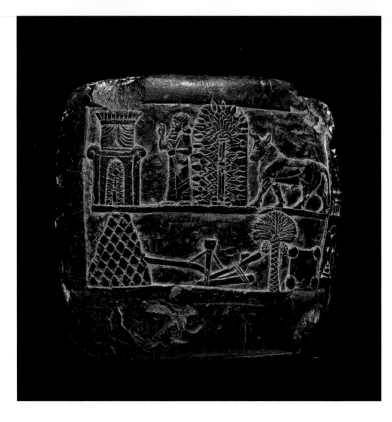

the late 600s and early 500s B.C. Scholars estimate that by 550 B.C., the story was somewhere between two and three centuries old, thereby dating it to the period of 850 to 750 B.C. Keep in mind that the Neo-Babylonians of the sixth century B.C. had at best a foggy, very imprecise idea of the actual progression of historical events in that earlier era.

Thanks to modern archaeology, however, historians have a fairly good grasp of the main events of that period. Sure enough, a rough historical sketch of those centuries matches the thematic thrust of the myth almost perfectly. In general, Babylon suffered significantly at the hands of several Assyrian conquerors in that period. By circa 823 B.C., when Shamshi-Adad V ascended Assyria's throne, Babylon had already undergone about three centuries of economic troubles and on-and-off political domination by outside aggressors. In 814 B.C. Shamshi-Adad then made matters worse by invading Babylonia, burning many of its villages, seizing the capital, and skinning alive its king, Marduk-balassu-iqbi. In the following century another Assyrian monarch, Tiglathpi-leser III, merged the remnants of Babylonia with Assyria and made himself king of the Babylonians. Finally, the powerful Assyrian conqueror Sennacherib (reigned 705 to 681 B.C.) devastated the city of Babylon, reducing it almost to a ghost town for perhaps more than a decade. (Sennacherib's son, Esarhaddon, rebuilt the city.)

The later Babylonians therefore had a horrifying but vague memory of the decimation of their capital. But they lacked systematic, accurate records of what had happened and when. So over time their oral retellings filled in the blanks, so to speak, by crediting the war god Erra with the destruction, showing that at least some Babylonian myths were, more or less, highly distorted historical records.

Atrahasis and the Great Flood

A different sort of historical event was the subject of the most famous of all Babylonian myths—the story of the great flood. It is sometimes called the myth or story of Atrahasis, after its main character.

The tale seems to have originated in Sumer in the third millennium B.C., and from there it passed, in several different versions, to the Babylonians and other peoples who arose in Mesopotamia in the millennium that followed. The most substantial written version, of which about 80 percent survives, was produced by a scribe in Babylon in the early 1600s B.C.

In the tale Atrahasis was the ruler of a Sumerian city not far from Uruk. One day Ea, the deity of wisdom and freshwater, visited Atrahasis in a dream and informed him that the god of storms, Ellil, was angry at human beings and planned to wipe them out in an enormous flood. Ea explained that he was warning the king about the coming catastrophe because he did not want to see humans destroyed. "Dismantle [your] house," the god told the man, "build a boat, reject [your] possessions, and save living things."[41]

Atrahasis did as Ea had instructed. He fashioned a large boat and, according to the third of the three tablets on which the original story was carved, he gathered together all sorts of animals. These included the birds "that fly in the sky, cattle, [and] wild animals." The man also "put his family on board." Not long afterward, the flood Ea had predicted arrived with great ferocity. "The winds were raging even as [Atrahasis] went up and cut through the rope [to release] the boat. . . . No one could see anyone else, they could not be recognized in the catastrophe. The Flood roared like a bull, like a wild

The biblical story of Noah's ark and the great flood may have been inspired by the tale of Atrahasis and the great Babylonian flood.

Did Tsunamis Cause the Flood?

One of the more recent theories about the great flood described in the Babylonian myths blames the disaster on the impact of a small comet or asteroid in the Indian Ocean, near the island of Madagascar, around 2800 B.C. According to archaeologist Bruce Masse, of the Los Alamos National Laboratory in New Mexico, and other researchers, the impact caused giant tsunamis to form. These moved across the Indian Ocean, swept into the Persian Gulf, and crashed ashore in Sumer. An impact crater that may be the origin of the event was discovered on the sea floor a few hundred miles southeast of Madagascar by Dallas Abbott of the Lamont-Doherty Earth Observatory. Dubbed Burckle Crater, it is about 18 miles (29km) across. Masse, Abbott, and other scientists have called attention to some oddly shaped dune deposits on the southern coast of Madagascar that seem to have been created by giant waves. If the impact can be verified and the timing in the early third millennium B.C. proves correct, there is virtually no doubt that the Sumerians would have witnessed at least some flooding.

ass screaming the winds [howled]. The darkness was total, there was no sun."[42]

The disaster killed all the humans and animals that were not in Atrahasis's boat. Discovering that vessel and its survivors, Ellil was angry with Ea for interfering with his destructive plans. From this point on in the third tablet, there are several lacunae (missing sections), so it is hard to tell how the story ended. However, a different Mesopotamian myth about the flood says that Ea persuaded Ellil that saving the humans had been a good idea. So Ellil "repented of his wrath against mankind." To Atrahasis and his wife, he said, "From this day on, you two shall be as gods and you shall live forever. . . . You alone, of all mankind, shall have the precious gift of everlasting life, and you shall walk forever in the garden of the gods."[43]

A Traumatic Memory?

Archaeologists who dug at sites in the Middle East in the early twentieth century were fascinated by the myth of Atrahasis and other similar flood tales from that region. The most famous of all, of course, was the story of the flood in

In the 1920s archaeologist Charles Leonard Woolley, second from right, discovered what he thought was evidence of a great flood at ancient Ur in Mesopotamia.

the biblical book of Genesis, in which Atrahasis's character is called Noah. Some scholars felt such tales were only fables and that no universal giant flood had occurred. But others argued that these myths might well be based on a real, historical catastrophe that left behind memories in the form of scattered oral stories that were eventually written down. In this view, as Stephanie Dalley phrases it, "All these flood stories may be explained as deriving from the one Mesopotamian original, used in travellers' tales for over two thousand years, along the great caravan routes of Western Asia [and subsequently] translated, embroidered, and adapted according to local tastes to give [numerous] divergent versions, a few of which have come down to us."[44]

Assuming that a real flood had taken place and triggered the spread of these myths, experts looked for evidence of such a large-scale disaster. Among them was the noted English archaeologist Charles Leonard Woolley (1880–1960). He was digging at the site of ancient Ur (southeast of Uruk) in the 1920s when he found an 8-foot-thick layer (2.4m) of soil lying between two horizontal levels of houses and other human artifacts. Woolley proposed that a large inflow of water had deposited the sandwiched soil layer. In the years that followed, excavators working at other southern Mesopotamian sites discovered similar soil deposits that seemed to have been laid down by flowing water. However, close examination showed that most of these soil layers had been deposited by small, localized floods that had occurred randomly over the course of many centuries. So it was clear that this evidence was not related to a universal flood of large-scale proportions. What was needed was proof of a single, immense natural catastrophe that could have spawned all of the various Middle Eastern myths of a "great flood."

The first credible evidence of this kind emerged in 1998. A group of scientists, including Columbia University's William Ryan and Walter Pitman, focused attention on the Black Sea and its immediate environs. Prior to the sixth millennium (5000s) B.C., the evidence showed, that waterway was very different than it is today. Much of it was dry land, and the rest was a shallow freshwater lake. At the time, the higher-level waters of the Mediterranean and Aegean Seas were held back by an enormous natural earthen dam that plugged what is now the Bosporus strait.

In about 5600 B.C., that blockage collapsed, allowing vast torrents of salt water to pour into the lower-lying Black Sea region. As many as 60,000 square miles (155,399 sq. km) of dry land were submerged in only a few weeks or so. The thousands of farmers and others who then lived along

The Fertile Crescent

A number of scholars think that before the formation of the Black Sea in the disaster of circa 5600 B.C., that region was the northernmost sector of the so-called Fertile Crescent. A wide arc of well-watered foothills and valleys that bordered the Mesopotamian plains in the north, the crescent was where agriculture began between 10,000 and 9000 B.C.

the lake's shores either drowned or fled for their lives. The tsunami-like walls of water formed "a thundering flume twisting and churning with rubble," Ryan and Pitman later wrote.

> Ten cubic miles of water poured through [the newly formed strait] each day, two hundred times what flows over Niagara Falls, enough to cover Manhattan Island each day to a depth of over half a mile. . . .

> It is hard to imagine the terror of those farmers, forced from their fields by an event they could not understand, a force of such incredible violence that it was as if the collected fury of all the gods was being hurled at them.[45]

According to this scenario, the refugees who had been displaced by the flood scattered in all directions. Of these, an undetermined number headed southeastward and ended up on the Mesopotamian plains. They carried with them the traumatic memory of the cataclysmic flood event, which continued to pass along orally through the generations that followed.

Other theories have since been advanced to explain the enigmatic flood legends of the Middle East. An intriguing one involves the impact of a small comet in the Indian Ocean, which supposedly generated giant tsunamis that flooded parts of Mesopotamia via the Persian Gulf. As of 2012, no one knows if any of these proposed natural events actually gave rise to the myths in question.

CHAPTER 5

Babylonian Myths' Impact on Western Society

B abylonian mythology's influence on Western civilization has been significant, although not so immediately obvious to most people. Indeed, at first glance it might seem that the Greek and Roman myths had a far larger impact on later Western societies than the Mesopotamian myths did. After all, the names of Greco-Roman gods, heroes, literary works, and objects are seemingly everywhere. They include the names of planets (Mars, Venus, Jupiter, Saturn, Neptune), cars (Saturn, Mercury, Odyssey, Electra), companies (Midas Muffler, Amazon.com), and products (Trident gum, Ajax cleanser, Nike shoes), to name only a few. Also, most modern novels and movies dealing with ancient myths have focused on those of the Greeks and Romans.

Nevertheless, the religion and myths of the Babylonians and other Mesopotamians have shaped modern society in profound, if more subtle, ways. Much of their influence has been on the Bible, which in turn has had a major impact on Judeo-Christian thought and society. This influence came about as the result of a short but crucial period of cultural contact between the early Hebrews and Babylonians. Historians and theologians call it the Babylonian Captivity. During most of the seventh century B.C., the Hebrew kingdom of

Judah had been a client state of the mighty Assyrian Empire. But after the Neo-Babylonians overthrew the Assyrian realm in the late 600s B.C., domination over Judah and other parts of Palestine transferred to Babylonia. The courageous Hebrews rebelled twice in the early 500s B.C. In response, the Babylonian king Nebuchadnezzar II sacked (looted) Jerusalem and deported all of Judah's nobles, along with other prominent citizens, to Babylon. The Hebrew prophet Jeremiah described how the invaders took "into exile from Jerusalem Jeconiah, the son of Jehoiakim, king of Judah, together with the princes of Judah, the craftsmen, and the smiths, and brought them to Babylon."[46]

The captives remained in Babylon from about 587 to 538 B.C. (when Persia's king Cyrus II, who had just conquered

A nineteenth-century woodcut depicts the sack of Jerusalem by Babylonian king Nebuchadnezzar II, who forced Judah's nobles into exile in Babylon.

Babylon, allowed them to return to Palestine). During those years in exile, the Hebrews encountered Babylonian religious concepts and myths. Some of these myths and concepts became very familiar to Hebrew intellectuals and writers, a few of whom composed some of the books of the Old Testament during or shortly after this period.

Atrahasis, Utnapishtim, and Noah

The influence of Babylonian myths on the Old Testament writers can be seen in the first book in the Bible, Genesis. In the past four decades, the vast majority of biblical scholars—Jewish, Christian, and nonreligious ones alike—have reached agreement on when Genesis was composed. They say that it was either written in its entirety or edited and expanded during and/or in the years directly following the Babylonian Captivity. This explains the prominence given to the story of Noah and the flood in the early portions of Genesis. Its writers had heard flood stories while captive in Babylon. One was that of Atrahasis, who had been instructed by a god to build a large boat and to place within it animals of all kinds. A very similar flood tale was told by the character Utnapishtim in a section of the Gilgamesh epic. In it Utnapishtim told Gilgamesh about how he had been warned about the coming flood by a god and had built a boat on which he, his family, and members of each animal species had survived. There is complete agreement among biblical scholars that Noah's story was based directly on these Babylonian versions of the great flood.

It is only natural to ask why these Hebrew writers borrowed the main elements of a Babylonian myth for their own account of early human history. To understand, one must first consider the varied meanings of the word *myth*. Today most people think about myths as old stories that are based on fantasy or misconceptions or are otherwise false. There is a tendency for people to believe that their own religious stories are historical and true, whereas those of other religions are myths and untrue.

But neither the Babylonians nor the Hebrews nor any other ancient peoples viewed myths that way. To them, all myths about earlier times were largely true accounts of real

Most scholars now agree that the story of Noah and the flood was written by Jewish writers while or shortly after they were held captive in Babylon.

historical events. The Hebrew captives, who were monotheists (believing in only one god), did not believe in the existence of the Babylonians' multiple gods, of course. But that did not mean they dismissed all the Babylonian myths as necessarily false. In fact, the Hebrews were well aware that Babylonian civilization was far older than their own, and they very likely assumed that their captives had access to valuable ancient records. There was no reason for the Hebrews to suppose that the great flood described in Atrahasis's tale was untrue. So they readily adopted it, in the process changing the leading character's name to Noah.

Several of the close parallels between the Babylonian and Hebrew versions of the flood story have been noted—among them a god warning the main character about the oncoming disaster; the order to build a boat, often called an ark; and the collection of specimens of existing animals to be saved. In another similarity, both Utnapishtim and Noah released a dove from the ark in order to test whether the waters had receded enough to expose any dry land. One of the closest parallels between the Babylonian and Hebrew accounts is the reason that the deity decided to destroy humanity: Namely, the human race had gotten out of hand. The Atrahasis story says, "The country became too wide, the people too numerous. The country was as noisy as a bellowing bull. The gods grew restless at their noise. Ellil [told the other gods], 'The noise of mankind has become too much. Sleep cannot overtake me because of their racket.'"[47] In comparison, Genesis reads, "When men began to multiply on the face of the ground . . . the Lord saw that the wickedness of man was great in the earth. . . . And the Lord was sorry that he had made man on the earth, and it grieved him to his heart. So the Lord said . . . 'I am sorry that I have made them.'"[48]

It is important to emphasize that in the twenty-five or so centuries following the Babylonian Captivity, Noah's story in Genesis became immortalized throughout the Western world. The stories of Atrahasis and Utnapishtim, however, did not. They were largely forgotten after the fall of Babylonian civilization in the sixth and fifth centuries B.C. So for a long time virtually no one knew that the Judeo-Christian story of the great flood was based on Babylonian myths. It was not until the late 1800s that archaeological discoveries in the Middle East brought the Babylonian tales to light once more. Their translations rocked Western literary and religious circles because they showed definitively that the flood story in Genesis was not original.

The Hebrews' Plight Captured in Paint

The Babylonian Captivity is the subject of a magnificent painting by noted French painter James J. Tissot (1836–1902). Dating from around 1900, the work shows thousands of Hebrews being driven out of Jerusalem by Babylonian soldiers.

Mourning Jerusalem's Fall

The biblical book of Lamentations presents the prophet Jeremiah's sadness and mourning over the recent sacking (looting) of Jerusalem by the Babylonians and the deportation of large numbers of Hebrews to Babylon. Jeremiah said in part that the city's

> gates have sunk into the ground [and] her king and princes are among the nations [in other countries, having been deported]. The law is no more, and [Judah's] prophets obtain no vision from [have lost contact with] the Lord. The [Hebrew] elders . . . sit on the ground in silence. They have cast dust on their heads and put on sackcloth [traditional acts of mourning]. The maidens of Jerusalem have bowed their heads to the ground. My eyes are spent with weeping. My soul is in tumult [turmoil]. My heart is poured out in grief because of the destruction of the daughter of my people, because infants and babies faint in the streets of the city. . . . In the dust of the streets lie the young and the old, my maidens and my young men have fallen by the sword . . . [slaughtered] without mercy.

Lamentations 2:9–11, 21. Revised Standard Edition.

The book of Lamentations in the Bible describes the prophet Jeremiah's sadness and mourning over the fall of Jerusalem and the deportation of large numbers of Hebrews to Babylon.

Other Biblical Parallels

The flood story was not the only Babylonian myth that later inspired the writers of some of the books of the Bible. Indeed, the Old Testament contains numerous events and anecdotes similar to those found in Mesopotamian tales. There are parallels, for example, between the story of Sargon, the Akkadian king who unified the Sumerian cities and established the world's first empire in the third millennium B.C., and the biblical stories of the prophet Moses. The myth about the infant Sargon being placed in a reed basket and tossed into a river was still very popular in the Middle East during the Babylonian Captivity. It appears certain that the biblical book of Exodus was penned during or shortly after this time. So it is perhaps not surprising that its writers incorporated Sargon's earliest adventure into their narrative of the young Moses.

Egypt's pharaoh had ordered that all Hebrew male babies be killed, the biblical version goes. So Moses's mother "hid him [for] three months. And when she could hide him no longer, she took for him a basket made of bulrushes [reeds] and she put the child in it and placed it among the reeds at the [Nile] river's brink."[49] Shortly afterward, the pharaoh's daughter, who was bathing in the river, found the baby and brought him into the palace, where he was subsequently raised as an Egyptian. In Sargon's version, Sargon recalls that "the river carried me to Akki, the water carrier. [He] raised me as his own son [and] I was beloved by Ishtar, [so] I became the king."[50]

The similarities between the stories of creation of the world in the *Enuma Elish* and Genesis are also striking. The Babylonian creation story begins with the words, "When the height of heaven was not named, and the earth beneath did not yet bear a name, [there was only] the primeval Apsu, who begat them, and chaos, Tiamat, the mother of them both, [and] their waters were mingled together."[51] Genesis says, "The earth was without form and void, and darkness was upon the face of the deep, and the Spirit of God was moving over the face of the waters."[52] In both cases earth had not yet appeared. It "did not yet bear a name" in the Babylonian version and "was without form" in the biblical

The myth of King Sargon being found in a reed basket as a child closely parallels the biblical story of the infant Moses being plucked from the Nile by the pharoah's daughter (pictured).

one. However, in each version there is a large expanse of water—the "Apsu" in one and the "deep" in the other. Scholar Marc A. Kroll points out:

> When comparing Genesis [and the] Enuma Elish, one can see that at the beginning of both narratives, there are natural forces of water that are already in existence prior to creation. Just as Apsu and Tiamat are primordial forces of fresh and saline water in the Enuma Elish, the *tehom* or the "deep" in Genesis is most likely primordial, because it is there before God begins the process of creation. God never creates it. Ever since the medieval period there has been a growing consensus among biblical scholars that God did not create the world *ex nihilo* or out "of nothing," because the

tehom was already in existence and the "wind of God swept over the water."[53]

It is also revealing that the Hebrew word used here for the "deep," *tehom*, is extremely close to the Akkadian name Tiamat. In fact, linguists believe that they are cognate, or deriving from a common source. This is not surprising, since both ancient Akkadian and ancient Hebrew were Semitic languages, which had a common ancestral tongue. These and other parallels between the two accounts show that the Hebrew version, though not by any means identical to, was nevertheless strongly influenced by the Babylonian one.

In addition, it has been established that the biblical description of the Garden of Eden was based in large part on Dilmun, the paradise from the myth of Ea and Ninhursag. Both the Garden of Eden and Dilmun were wet with

Most biblical scholars now believe that the biblical description of the Garden of Eden was based on the Babylonian creation of Dilmun. The geographical descriptions of their locations are similar.

water and lush with trees and other vegetation. Moreover, the writers of Genesis did not even attempt to hide the fact that the place they were describing was in or near Babylonia. They said that four rivers flowed beside Eden, the third and fourth of which were the Hiddekel and the Euphrates. The Euphrates, of course, flowed directly through Babylonia. As for the Hiddekel, scholars concur that it was the Euphrates's sister river, the Tigris. (The early Semitic name for the Tigris was the Idiklat, and the Hebrews came to call it the Hiddekel.) There can be no doubt, therefore, that the authors of Genesis had the Babylonian Dilmun in mind when setting the scene for God's creation of humans.

Novels and Graphic Novels

These and other parallels between Babylonian mythology and the Bible demonstrate how ancient stories of pagan (non-Christian) gods indirectly enriched the religious writings and ideas of the Judeo-Christian West. For the most part, the long process in which this cultural transference took place was subtle. It was generally known only to a few scholars and interested nonscholars.

In contrast, during the past century some characters from the Babylonian myths became well known to a broader public audience through their appearance in various aspects or genres of pop culture. Among the earliest examples of these genres was the novel. For instance, German novelist Hans Henny Jahnn's *River Without Shores* (1950) is a masterfully told story of two male friends whose relationship mirrors that of Gilgamesh and Enkidu in the *Epic of Gilgamesh*.

Later, in 1984, the great science-fiction writer Robert Silverberg published his novel *Gilgamesh the King*. It retells the story in the ancient epic in fairly realistic terms and allows the reader to decide whether some of the more fantastic elements are the result of intervention by the gods. Silverberg's sequel, the novella *Gilgamesh in the Outback* (1986), won the coveted Hugo Award for outstanding science fiction. Another popular science-fiction and fantasy writer, Jane Lindskold, also explored the characters Gilgamesh and Enkidu. In her novels *Changer* (1998) and *Legends Walking* (1999), they are among the many disguises of, or identities taken on by, the

Athanor, beings who have roamed the earth and intervened in human affairs for thousands of years.

Another literary genre—one often less reputable but no less popular than traditional novels—that has explored the characters of Babylonian mythology is the comic book or graphic novel. Writer-artist Matt Wagner's *Mage* series is a popular example. In *Mage II: The Hero Defined*, the main character, a restless young man named Kevin Matchstick, discovers that he was Gilgamesh in the distant past. Another example is Argentine artist Lucho Olivera's ongoing series *Gilgamesh the Immortal*. It deals with an ancient king who encounters an extraterrestrial being that uses technology to make the man immortal. The most prolific and perhaps most popular of all comic book companies—Marvel Comics—also features an ongoing character based on Gilgamesh. In this case he is one of the so-called Eternals, a group of superheroes charged with defending earth against any and all invaders.

Music, Theater, and Video Games

Among the several other areas of art and culture that have featured Babylonian myths are music, theater, and video games. In the musical genre, at least three operas have been based on the *Epic of Gilgamesh*. Particularly notable is Italian composer Franco Battiato's 1992 work *Gilgamesh*. The latter is also the title of a 2010 album by the Australian pop music duo Gypsy and the Cat. In addition, several ancient Babylonian characters, including Sargon, Hammurabi, and Gilgamesh, appear in the lyrics of the 2007 song "The Mesopotamians" by the American alternative rock band They Might Be Giants.

Onstage, Gilgamesh was one of the three characters in Rory Winston's *Turn Left at Gilgamesh*, which opened Off-Off-Broadway in New York City in March 1990. The play uses humor to comment on human foibles by showing

Gilgamesh on the Radio

In 1954 Douglas G. Bridson presented his radio play *The Quest of Gilgamesh* in a special broadcast on England's BBC. This show introduced the ancient Babylonian character to the people of Britain, few of whom had heard of him before that time.

Mesopotamian civilization appearing mainly by accident. Later, in 2007, playwright Blake Bowden's *Gilgamesh in Uruk: GI in Iraq* premiered at the Performance Gallery in Cincinnati, Ohio. It involves some American solders at a U.S. military base in Iraq who end up role-playing some ancient Babylonian characters to work out their frustrations. One reviewer commented that Bowden "has found the universal elements within this ancient tale and translated them into amusing and thoughtful episodes that teach Gilgamesh, and the audience, lessons about leading a satisfying life. Along the way, we see the true value of storytelling."[54]

Possibly the most popular of all pop culture renderings of Babylonian mythical characters have been those in video games. Among them, the *Babylonian Castle Saga* series, created by Masanobu Endo, has proved highly successful. It

Gilgamesh Rocks?

The highly effective lyrics to "The Mesopotamians," a song by the group They Might Be Giants, start out by identifying the band's members as the well-known ancient Mesopotamian figures Sargon, the Akkadian conqueror; Hammurabi, the Babylonian lawgiver; Ashurbanipal, the ruthless Assyrian monarch; and Gilgamesh, the mythical king who searched for the secret of immortality. As the song continues, these four names are repeated several times. There is also a line that mentions scratching words into clay, an obvious reference to the ancient Mesopotamian writing system known as cuneiform, in which scribes made impressions in moist clay tablets. Another apt reference to ancient Mesopotamia in the song is a description of old buildings crumbling into the sand, a natural process that has been ongoing for many centuries in the region. Still another evocative line mentions the hot sun causing cracks to appear in the ground. Parts of ancient Mesopotamia did indeed get very hot when the sun was high in the sky in the summer months.

originally consisted of four separate games—*The Tower of Druaga*, *The Return of Ishtar*, *The Quest of Ki*, and *The Blue Crystal Rod*. In the first game the hero Gilgamesh rescues a maiden named Ki from a nasty demon, Druaga. The other games then pick up the story line where this one leaves off (except for *The Quest of Ki*, which is a prequel to the first game). In addition, the goddess Tiamat, or deities or creatures based on her, have figured prominently in several video games, including Vigil Games' *Darksiders*, which so far has sold over 1 million copies worldwide.

Actors portray Gilgamesh and Enkidu in a 2002 theatrical presentation of the Gilgamesh epic in Austria.

He Is Among Us

Of all the ancient Babylonian characters portrayed in pop culture today, clearly Gilgamesh is by far the most popular and most often explored and exploited. In the words of Theodore Ziolkowski, a professor of comparative literature at Princeton University:

> Apart from novels, plays, poems, operas, and paintings, the ancient Babylonian hero shows up in children's books, *animes*, comic books, and video games. Within the past decade the epic has won its place in the standard

anthologies of world literature and has become a staple in college courses in literature and religion. . . .

In almost a hundred manifestations of [modern pop culture], the epic of Gilgamesh constitutes a finely tuned [measuring instrument] that registers many of the major intellectual, social, and moral upheavals of the past hundred years, from the religious controversies of the early twentieth century, by way of the search for eternal spiritual values transcending the decline of Western civilization following two world wars, to the struggle for recognition among previously marginalized groups, notably gays and feminists, and eventually to environmental concerns for planet Earth. . . . Wherever one looks today, and in the most varied manifestations, Gilgamesh is very much among us.[55]

Four cylinder seals and imprints with representations of Gilgamesh and Enkidu made around 2500 B.C. from the National Museum of Iraq. Forty-five hundred years later, Gilgamesh still lives.

Such widespread popularity is nothing less than amazing when one considers that Gilgamesh had been largely forgotten over the centuries. Not until shortly before the

Gilgamesh on Television

The *Epic of Gilgamesh* and its characters have proved to be widely popular in various artistic and cultural media in recent years. Television has been one such medium. For example, in a 1991 episode of *Star Trek: The Next Generation* titled "Darmok," Captain Picard of the starship *Enterprise* recites parts of Gilgamesh's story to the captain of an alien space vessel. Because this particular race of beings, the Tamarians, communicates mainly through allegory (expression of ideas through symbolic figures, actions, or stories), this helps to open a dialogue between the two races. The character and/or tale of Gilgamesh was also explored in episodes of the TV series *Highlander: The Series* and *Hercules: The Legendary Journeys*, as well as the animated *The Secret Saturdays*.

turn of the twentieth century did reliable translations of his epic story become available. Moreover, only after World War II (1939–1945) did that work become broadly known and begin to be studied in college and university courses. What has made the myth so compelling to so many people is that it deals with a number of universal questions and truths that have haunted humanity for generation after generation since the rise of civilization. As scholar Andrew George puts it, the story was and remains "about the fear of death." He adds:

> In examining the human longing for life eternal, it tells of one man's heroic struggle against death [and] of his eventual realization that the only immortality he may expect is the enduring name afforded by leaving behind some lasting achievement. [The story also] offers many profound insights into the human condition, into life and death and the truths that touch us all, [including a] man's responsibilities to his family . . . the benefits of civilization over savagery . . . the rewards of friendship, [and] the nobility of heroic enterprise.[56]

It is no wonder, then, that Gilgamesh has touched modern society's heart far more than any other mythical Mesopotamian figure. True, in the original story he was in part a failure because he found but then lost the means of gaining eternal life. Yet through his extensive use by modern novelists, composers, artists, and others, he has triumphed in the end by managing to attain a very different kind of immortality—everlasting fame as a hero of epic proportions. The ancient Babylonians were well aware of his heroic stature. After all, they admired him enough to eagerly tell and retell his story for more than a hundred generations. What they could never have anticipated was the new life Gilgamesh, Ishtar, and other popular characters from that antique culture would later enjoy in television, video games, and other electronic media—a brand of magic that lay far beyond their wildest imaginings.

Introduction: No Sense of History

1. Jennifer Westwood. *Gilgamesh and Other Babylonian Tales*. New York: Coward-McCann, 1970, p. 10.
2. Stephanie Dalley, ed. and trans. *Myths from Mesopotamia*. New York: Oxford University Press, 2000, pp. xviii–xix.
3. H.W.F. Saggs. *Babylonians*. Berkeley: University of California Press, 2000, p. 32.
4. Stephen Bertman. *Handbook to Life in Ancient Mesopotamia*. New York: Facts On File, 2003, p. 149.
5. Samuel N. Kramer. *Cradle of Civilization*. New York: Time-Life, 1978, p. 108.

Chapter 1: Babylonian Preservation of Gods and Myths

6. Karen Rhea Nemet-Nejat. *Daily Life in Ancient Mesopotamia*. Peabody, MA: Hendrickson, 2002, p. 31.
7. Norman Bancroft Hunt. *Historical Atlas of Ancient Mesopotamia*. New York: Facts On File, 2004, p. 70.
8. Cyril J. Gadd. "Sargon of Akkad." Third Millennium Library. www .third-millennium-library.com /readinghall/GalleryofHistory /Ancient-People/SARGON.htm.
9. Henrietta McCall. *Mesopotamian Myths*. Austin: University of Texas Press, 1990, p. 36.
10. Quoted in Herodotus. *The Histories*. Translated by Aubrey de Sélincourt. New York: Penguin, 2003, pp. 116–117.
11. Kramer. *Cradle of Civilization*, pp. 99–100.
12. Saggs. *Babylonians*, p. 35.
13. Kramer. *Cradle of Civilization*, p. 102.

Chapter 2: Searching for the Beginnings of Things

14. George A. Barton. "New Babylonian Material Concerning Creation and Paradise." *American Journal of Theology*, October 1917, p. 571.
15. Kramer. *Cradle of Civilization*, p. 108.
16. Gateways to Babylon. *Enki and Ninhursag*. Adaptation. www.gate waystobabylon.com/myths/texts /retellings/enkininhur.htm.
17. Gateways to Babylon. *Enki and Ninhursag*.
18. Tikya Frymer-Kensky. "Agricultural Fertility and the Sacred Marriage."

www.gatewaystobabylon.com. (Click on "Essays" and then on the title above.)

19. L.W. King, trans. *Enuma Elish*. Internet Sacred Text Archive. www .sacred-texts.com/ane/enuma.htm.

20. Micha F. Lindemans. "Anu." Encyclopedia Mythica. www.pantheon .org/articles/a/anu.html.

21. King. *Enuma Elish*.

22. King. *Enuma Elish*.

23. Kramer. *Cradle of Civilization*, pp. 104–105.

24. Electronic Text Corpus of Sumerian Literature. *Enmerkar and the Lord of Aratta*. http://etcsl.orinst .ox.ac.uk/section1/tr1823.htm.

25. Electronic Text Corpus of Sumerian Literature. *Enmerkar and the Lord of Aratta*.

26. Gateways to Babylon. "The Exploits of Ninurta." www.gatewaystobab ylon.com/myths/texts/ninurta /exploitninurta.htm.

Chapter 3: Quests for the Secrets of Immortality

27. John Gray. *Near Eastern Mythology*. New York: Peter Bedrick, 1985, p. 26.

28. Maureen G. Kovacs, John Maier, and John Gardner, trans. *Epic of Gilgamesh. Tablet 8*. MythHome. www.mythome.org/Gilgamesh .html.

29. Kovacs, Maier, Gardner. *Epic of Gilgamesh. Tablet 10*.

30. Richard Cowen. "The Bronze Age." MyGeologyPage. http://my geologypage.ucdavis.edu/cowen /~gel115/115ch4.html.

31. Kovacs, Maier, Gardner. *Epic of Gilgamesh. Tablet 11*.

32. Gwendolyn Leick. *The Babylonians*. London: Routledge, 2003, pp. 154–155.

33. Quoted in Dalley. *Myths from Mesopotamia*, p. 186.

34. Quoted in Dalley. *Myths from Mesopotamia*, p. 187.

35. Mario Liverani. *Myth and Politics in Ancient Near Eastern Historiography*. Ithaca, NY: Cornell University Press, 2004, p. 17.

Chapter 4: The Inevitability of Conflict and Calamity

36. S.H. Hooke. *Middle Eastern Mythology*. New York: Dover, 2004, p. 19.

37. E.A. Speiser, trans. *The Descent of Ishtar*. Gateways to Babylon. www .gatewaystobabylon.com/myths /texts/classic/ishtardesc.htm.

38. Bertman. *Handbook to Life in Ancient Mesopotamia*, p. 159.

39. Gateways to Babylon. *Erra and Ishum*. Adaptation. www.gatewaysto babylon.com/myths/texts/classic /erraishum.htm.

40. Gateways to Babylon. *Erra and Ishum*.

41. Quoted in Dalley. *Myths from Mesopotamia*, pp. 29–30.

42. Quoted in Dalley. *Myths from Mesopotamia*, p. 31.

43. Quoted in Westwood. *Gilgamesh and Other Babylonian Tales*, p. 34.

44. Dalley. *Myths from Mesopotamia*, p. 7.

45. William Ryan and Walter Pitman. *Noah's Flood: The New Scientific Discoveries About the Event That Changed History*. New York: Simon and Schuster, 2000, pp. 234–235.

Chapter 5: Babylonian Myths' Impact on Western Society

46. Jeremiah 24:1. Revised Standard Edition.

47. Quoted in Dalley. *Myths from Mesopotamia*, p. 21.

48. Genesis 6:1–7. Revised Standard Edition.

49. Exodus 2:2–3. Revised Standard Edition.

50. Quoted in Otto Rank. *The Myth of the Birth of the Hero: A Psychological Interpretation of Mythology*. Baltimore: Johns Hopkins University Press, 2004, pp. 12–13.

51. King. *Enuma Elish*.

52. Genesis 1:2. Revised Standard Edition.

53. Marc A. Kroll. "Judaism Ultimate Reality and Divine Beings." Patheos. www.patheos.com/Library /Judaism/Beliefs/Ultimate-Reality -and-Divine-Beings.html.

54. Rick Pender. "Onstage Review: Gilgamesh in Uruk (GI in Iraq)." *City Beat*, October 3, 2007. www .citybeat.com/cincinnati/article -3289-onstage-review-gilga mesh-in-uruk-%28gi-in-iraq%29 .html.

55. Theodore Ziolkowski. "Gilgamesh: An Epic Obsession." Berfrois, November 1, 2011. www.berfrois .com/2011/11/theodore-ziolkowski -gilgamesh.

56. Andrew George, trans. *The Epic of Gilgamesh: A New Translation*. New York: Penguin, 1999, p. xiii.

agrarian: Having to do with agriculture.

antiquity: Ancient times.

Assyriology: The study or intellectual discipline of ancient Mesopotamia.

bronze: An alloy, or mixture, of the metals copper and tin.

client state: A country or other political unit that owes allegiance or is subordinate in some way to another.

cognate: Deriving from a common source.

consort: A spouse, mate, or companion.

diorite: A very hard rock often used in ancient times as a tool or weapon.

dynasty: A family line of rulers.

ex nihilo: Appearing out of nothing.

lacunae (singular is lacuna): Missing parts or sections.

monotheist: Someone who believes in a single, all-powerful god.

Neolithic: Existing in an era when people practiced agriculture but still used stone tools and weapons; as a noun, it refers to the Neolithic Age.

numina (singular is numen): Invisible supernatural forces.

pantheon: A group of gods worshipped by a people or nation.

parable: A fable or other story, usually having a moral lesson.

parsu: In ancient Babylonia and Assyria, rules governing nature and human relations; the Sumerians called them *me*.

primeval: Extremely ancient.

procession: A solemn parade, most often religious in nature.

scribe: In the ancient world, a person who used his or her reading and writing skills in some professional capacity.

tsunami: A huge wave set in motion by landslides, earthquakes, or other large-scale natural events.

vizier: A high-level political administrator or other government leader.

Books

Stephen Bertman. *Handbook to Life in Ancient Mesopotamia*. New York: Facts On File, 2003. A fact-filled, easy-to-read guide to the region's peoples, leaders, religious beliefs and myths, social customs, languages, arts and crafts, and much more.

Jeremy Black et al., eds. *The Literature of Ancient Sumer*. New York: Oxford University Press, 2006. This is a comprehensive and useful collection of Sumerian literature of all types.

Stephanie Dalley, ed. and trans. *Myths from Mesopotamia*. New York: Oxford University Press, 2000. An impressive compilation of English translations of the major Mesopotamian myths.

Benjamin R. Foster, ed. *From Distant Days: Myths, Tales, and Poetry of Ancient Mesopotamia*. Bethesda, MD: CDL, 1995. A collection of easy-to-read translations of ancient Mesopotamian literature, suitable for junior high and high school students as well as general adult readers.

John Gray. *Near Eastern Mythology*. New York: Peter Bedrick, 1985. This synopsis of the major myths of the Mesopotamians and other ancient Near Eastern (Middle Eastern) peoples by a noted scholar is well written and authoritative.

Norman Bancroft Hunt. *Historical Atlas of Ancient Mesopotamia*. New York: Facts On File, 2004. Contains dozens of excellent maps helpful to those interested in ancient Mesopotamia.

Samuel N. Kramer. *Cradle of Civilization*. New York: Time-Life, 1978. Despite its age, this classic book written by the late scholar Samuel N. Kramer remains the best-ever short overview of ancient Mesopotamian civilization and religion.

Samuel N. Kramer. *The Sumerians: Their History, Culture, and Character*. Chicago: University of Chicago Press, 1982. This landmark study is one of the most comprehensive studies of Sumerian civilization available.

Gwendolyn Leick. *Mesopotamia: The Invention of the City*. New York: Penguin, 2001. In her detailed examination of key Mesopotamian cities, Leick, one of the foremost authorities on ancient Mesopotamia, discusses numerous aspects of the region's literature and myths.

Henrietta McCall. *Mesopotamian Myths*. Austin: University of Texas Press, 1990. A useful, easy-to-read general introduction to Mesopotamian mythology, with plenty of information on writing methods and other cultural aspects of the ancient peoples who held these stories dear.

Geraldine McCaughrean. *Gilgamesh*. Grand Rapids, MI: Eerdmans, 2002. This entertaining recent retelling of the famous Gilgamesh myth is aimed at younger readers and contains numerous handsome illustrations by David Parkins.

Stephen Mitchell, trans. *Gilgamesh*. New York: Free Press, 2004. An excellent recent English translation of the most famous and important of the ancient Mesopotamian myths.

Michael Roaf. *Cultural Atlas of Mesopotamia and the Ancient Near East*. New York: Facts On File, 1990. This well-illustrated book provides a useful synopsis of the main cultural aspects of the ancient Mesopotamian peoples.

H.W.F. Saggs. *Babylonians*. Berkeley: University of California Press, 2000. A first-rate scholar delivers an insightful overview of ancient Babylonian culture, society, and ideas.

Websites

Ancient Mesopotamia: Archaeology, Oriental Institute of the University of Chicago (http://oi.uchicago.edu/OI/MUS/ED/TRC/MESO/archaeology.html). This site features several links to brief but excellent articles about ancient Mesopotamia.

***Enuma Elish*, Internet Sacred Text Archive** (www.sacred-texts.com/ane/enuma.htm). L.W. King's translation of the famous Babylonian creation epic.

***Epic of Atrahasis*, Livius** (www.livius.org/as-at/atrahasis/atrahasis.html). Contains a translation of the surviving parts of this ancient Mesopotamian epic, which mentions the same great flood described in the Bible.

Hammurabi, Humanistic Texts (www.humanistictexts.org/hammurabi.htm). Contains excellent translations of many of the famous Babylonian ruler's laws.

Recent Cosmic Impacts on Earth, About.com: Archaeology (http://archaeology.about.com/od/climatechange/a/masse_king.htm). Archaeologist Thomas F. King summarizes recent theories about the impacts of comets and asteroids, one of which might have caused the disaster described in the Babylonian flood myth.

The Tablets Telling the Epic of Gilgamesh, MythHome (www.mythome.org/Gilgamesh.html). The home page for an excellent translation of Gilgamesh's epic tale, with which all ancient Mesopotamians were familiar.

INDEX

A

Adad. *See* Ishtar
Adapa (priest), 56–60, 58
   boat of, *57*
   myth of, as tale of hospitality, 59–61
Agog (rock warrior), 45
Akkad (Agade, city-state), 9, 20
Akkadian (language), 9
Akkadian myths/epics, 10
Akki (water carrier), 20, 83
Anu (deity), 39, 56–58
Anunnaki (Annunaki, minor gods), 29
Apsu (deity), 39–40
Ashurbanipal (Assyrian monarch), 23
Assyria, 9
Atrahasis (Sumerian ruler), 71–73

B

Babylon/Babylonian civilization, 7
   ancient city of, *24*
   Assyrian domination of, 22–23
   beginnings of, 16
   destruction of, 68-71, *69*
   influence of Sumerian culture on, 8
   under Kassites, 22
   location of, 13
   major characters in mythology of, *6*
   reconstruction of, *70*, 71
   tale of Erra's destruction of, 68–71
Babylonian Castle Saga series (Endo), 88–89

Babylonian gods
   evolution of, 25–27
   family tree of, *5*
   principal, 27, 29
Bible, 77
   See also Old Testament; *specific books*
Bowden, Blake, 88

C

Changer (Lindskold), 87
Creation myths, 33–34, 36
   Marduk's, 38–43
      parallels between Babylonian and
         Hebrew, 83–86
Cuneiform symbols, 39
Cuneiform tablets, *55*
   Akkadian, *9*, *44*
Cylinder seal/imprint, from Kassite
   period, *22*

D

Darius I (Persian monarch), 25
Death, Babylonian view of, 54–55
Demeter (Greek deity), 66
Diorite (mineral), 46
Dumuzi (deity), 56, 57

E

Ea (deity), 29, 36–37, *37*, 39–40, 56–57,
   58, 71–72, 73
Ellil (Enlil, deity), 27, 29, 71, 73

Endo, Masanobu, 88–89
Enkidu, 49, **50**, 51, 52, 55, 86, 87
    actor portraying, 87, *89*
Enmerkar and the Lord of Aratta (epic), 43
Enuma Elish (epic), 38–39, 83, 84
Epic of Gilgamesh, 47, 48
    flood tale in, 79
    novels based on, 86–87
    in popular culture, 89–91
Ereshkigal (deity), *63*, 65
Ereshkigal (queen of Underworld), 62–65,
    65
Eridu (city), 56, *60*, 64
Etana (Sumerian king), 55

F

Fertile Crescent, *5*, 71
Fertility/fertility myths, 36–38
    gods of, 67
The flood, 7, *72*, 73, *80*
    archeological evidence of, 74–76
    Atrahasis and, 71–73
    theory on cause of, 73

G

Garden of Eden, 86
Genesis, 39, 58, 74, 79
Geshtinanna (deity), 66
Gilgamesh, 43, *48*, *52*
    actor portraying, *89*
    on death of Enkidu, 52
    quest to find Utnapishtim, 50–51,
        53–54
    slaying bull of Ishtar, *50*
    See also Epic of Gilgamesh
Gilgamesh (Battiato), 87
Gilgamesh in the Outback (Silverberg), 86
Gilgamesh in Uruk: GI in Iraq (Bowden),
    88

Gilgamesh the Immortal (Olivera), 87
Gilgamesh the King (Silverberg), 86
Gizzida (deity), 56, 57

H

Hadad. *See* Ishtar
Hades (Greek deity), *66*
Hammurabi (Babylonian king)
    achievements of, 16–18, *19*
    law code of, 19
Hanging Gardens of Babylon, 23
Hebrews
    Babylonian captivity of, 77–79, 81
    Babylonian religious concepts adopted
        by, 29
    creation myths of, 83–86
    influence of Babylonian myths on,
        79–80
Herodotus, 11, 24–25
Hittites, 21–22

I

Igigi (divine laborers), 29
Ishtar (Adad, Hadad, Inanna; deity), 25,
    28, 29, 62, *65*
    Gilgamesh and, 49

J

Jahnn, Hans Henny, 86
Jeremiah (prophet), 82
Jerusalem, Babylonian sack of, *78*, 82, *82*

K

Kassites, 21–22

L

Lamashtu (female demon), 64
Lamentations, 82

Lebanon, 56
Legends Walking (Lindskold), 87
Lindskold, Jane, 87
Literature
    of high Babylonian culture, 18–20
    modern, Babylonian mythology in,
      86–87

M

Mage series (Wagner), 87
Marduk (deity), 27, 29, *40*, 41–43, *42*
    image of, 32–33, *33*
Mesopotamia, 8
    map of, *4*
Moses, 83, *84*
Music, Babylonian mythology in,
    87–88

N

Nabopolassar (Neo-Babylonian ruler),
    23
Nabu (deity), 23
Nebuchadnezzar II (Babylonian king),
    23, *78*
Neo-Babylonian Empire, 23
Neolithic era, 25
New Year's festival, 32
Ninhursag (deity), 36–37
Ninkurra (deity), 36
Ninlil (deity), 30
Ninsar (deity), 36
Ninurta and Agog (myth), 44–46
Nitocris (Neo-Babylonian queen),
    23–25
Noah, 7, 74, 79
Noah's ark, *15, 72*
Novels, Babylonian mythology in,
    86–87
Numina (supernatural forces), 25–26

O

Old Testament
    parallels between Babylonian myths
      and, 83–86
    See also specific books
Olivera, Lucho, 87

P

Parsu (divine regulations), 29–30
    tablet describing, *31*
Persephone (Greek deity), *66*
Pickax, 45
Pitman, Walter, 46, 74

Q

The Quest of Gilgamesh (radio play), 83

R

Religion/religious beliefs
    of ancient Mesopotamia, 25–27
    fertility as concern of, 38
    Sumerian, 17
River Without Shores (Jahnn), 86
Ryan, William, 46, 74

S

Sargon (Akkadian king), *21*, 83
    myths of, 20
Sargon (Babylonian king), 84
Sennacherib (Assyrian monarch), 71
Shamash (deity), 29, 55
Shamshi Adad V (Assyrian monarch),
    70
Siduri (deity), 51
Silverberg, Robert, 86
Sin (deity), 29, 30
Sumerian culture, 8

Sumerian King Lists, 20, 47, 55
Sumerian religion, 17

T

Tablet of Destinies, 41
Tammuz (deity), 45, 66, 67
Television, Babylonian mythology on, 90
Temple of Anu, *60*
"The Mesopotamians" (song), 87
They Might Be Giants (rock band), 87, 88
Thucydides, 11
Tiamat (deity), 39, 41, *42*
Tissot, James J., 81
Turn Left at Gilgamesh (Winston), 87

U

Underworld, 7, 54
  Ishtar's descent into, 62–66

Utnapishtim, 50, 51, 54, 79, 81

V

Video games, Babylonian mythology in,
  88–89

W

Wagner, Matt, 87
Winston, Rory, 87
Woolley, Charles Leonard, 74, *75*
The Wrath of Erra, 67–71

X

Xenophon, 11

Z

Ziggurats, 35, *35*

PICTURE CREDITS

Cover: © kated/Shutterstock.com

123 0832024 The Great Flood, 1860 (engraving), Spanish School, (19th century)/Private Collection/Index/The Bridgeman Art Library, 80

© Alfredo Dagli Orti/The Art Archive at Art Resource, NY, 18

© Alinari/Art Resource, NY, 85

© Ancient Art & Architecture Collection, Ltd/Alamy, 66

© AP Images/Stephan Trierenberg, 89

© Balage Balogh/Art Resource, NY, 24, 57, 60

© bpk, Berlin/Carl August Zscheckel/Art Resource, NY, 78

© Classic Image/Alamy, 37, 40, 50, 72

© DeA Picture Library/Art Resource, NY, 35

© DeA Picture Library/De Agostini/Getty Images, 74

© Erich Lessing/Art Resource, NY, 9, 19, 21, 22, 44, 48, 70

Gale, Cengage Learning, 4, 5, 6

Ishtar in Hades, illustration from 'Myths of Babylonia and Assyria' by Donald A. Makenzie, 1915 (colour litho), Wallcousins, Ernest (1883–1976) (after)/Private Collection/The Stapleton Collection/The Bridgeman Art Library, 65

Mighty was he to look upon, illustration from 'Myths and Legends of Babylonia and Assyria' by Lewis Spence, 1916 (colour litho), Paul, Evelyn (1870–1945)/Private Collection/The Stapleton Collection/The Bridgeman Art Library, 42

New Year's Day in Babylon, Jackson, Peter (1922-2003)/Private Collection/© Look and Learn/The Bridgeman Art Library, 33

© NGS Image Collection/The Art Archive at Art Resource, NY, 52

© North Wind Picture Archives/Alamy, 82

© Photoservice Electa/Laurent Lecat/Art Resource, NY, 15

© Roger Viollet Collection/Getty Images, 90

© Scala/Art Resource, NY, 28

Tablet relating the ritual sacrifices at the Temple of Anu in Uruk (Warka) copy of an ancient text of 3rd-1st century BC (clay), Mesopotamian/Louvre, Paris, France/Giraudon/The Bridgeman Art Library, 31

© The Trustees of the British Museum/Art Resource, NY, 55, 63, 69

© Universal History Archive/Getty Images, 84

ABOUT THE AUTHOR

Historian Don Nardo has written numerous acclaimed volumes about ancient civilizations and peoples. Among these are studies of the religious beliefs and myths of those peoples, including the Greeks, Romans, Egyptians, Sumerians, and others. Nardo also composes and arranges orchestral music. He resides with his wife, Christine, in Massachusetts.